Berlitz®

Brazilian Portuguese

phrase book & dictionary

Berlitz Publishing
New York

Contacting the Editors

Every effort has been made to provide accurate information in this publication, but changes are inevitable. The publisher cannot be responsible for any resulting loss, inconvenience or injury. We would appreciate it if readers would call our attention to any errors or outdated information. We also welcome your suggestions; if you come across a relevant expression not in our phrasebook, please contact us at: comments@berlitzpublishing.com

First Printing: 2014
Printed in China

Senior Commissioning Editor: Kate Drynan
Translation: Wordbank
Phonetic transcription: Wordbank
Design: Beverley Speight
Production Manager: Vicky Glover
Picture Researcher: Beverley Speight
Cover Photo: All photos Yadid Levy/APA.

Interior Photos: All photos Yadid Levy/APA except Britta Jaschinski/APA p47; Bev Speight/APA p148; iStockphoto p23,82,145,154,155,161,166

Contents

Food & Drink

People

Leisure Time

Special Requirements

In an Emergency

Dictionary

Pronunciation

This section is designed to make you familiar with the sounds of Brazilian Portuguese using our simplified phonetic transcription. You'll find the pronunciation of the Brazilian Portuguese letters and sounds explained below, together with their 'imitated' equivalents. This system is used throughout the phrase book; simply read the pronunciation as if it were English, noting any special rules below.

Please note that any syllables that should be stressed are indicated by underlining in the phonetics.

Brazilian Portuguese has four accent marks; acute (´), grave (`), circumflex (ˆ), and tilde (˜). Accent marks are used to indicate a stressed syllable, or to distinguish between words with the same spelling but with a different pronunciation and meaning: for example, **é** pronounced *eh* (meaning is) and **e** pronounced *ee* (meaning and).

Consonants

Letter	Approximate Pronunciation	Symbol	Example	Pronunciation
b	1. as in English	**b**	**bota**	*baw•tuh*
	2. between vowels, as in English but softer	**b**	**bebida**	*beh•bee•duh*
c	1. before e or i, like s in same	**s**	**centro**	*sehn•troh*
	2. like k in kit	**k**	**como**	*koh•moh*
ç	like s in same	**s**	**cabeça**	*kuh•beh•suh*
ch	like sh in shower	**sh**	**chave**	*shahvd*

Letter	Approximate Pronunciation	Symbol	Example	Pronunciation
d	1. as in English	**d**	**diário**	*dee•ah•ree•oo*
	2. like th in theater	**th**	**medo**	*meh•thoo*
g	1. before e or i, like s in pleasure	**zs**	**gelo**	*zseh•loo*
	2. before a, o or u, as in English	**g**	**guerra**	*geh•rruh*
h	always silent		**história**	*ee•staw•ree•uh*
j	like s in pleasure	**zs**	**juiz**	*zsoo•eezs*
l	1. as in English	**l**	**luz**	*looz*
	2. before h (lh), like ll in millions	**ly**	**milho**	*mee•lyoo*
m	1. as in English	**m**	**câmera**	*cuh•meh•ruh*
	2. at the end of a word, m is nasalized: see p10			
n	1. as in English	**n**	**caneta**	*kuh•neh•tah*
	2. before h (nh), like ny in canyon	**ny**	**banho**	*buh•nyoo*
qu	1. before e and i, like k in kite	**k**	**quente**	*kint*
	2. before a and o like qu in queen	**kw**	**qualidade**	*kwah•lee•dahd*
r	1. strongly trilled	**rr**	**rio**	*rree•oo*
	2. lightly trilled	**r**	**para**	*puh•ruh*
s	1. like s in same	**s**	**sua**	*soo•uh*
	2. between vowels, like z in zebra	**z**	**camisa**	*kuh•mee•zuh*

Letter	Approximate Pronunciation	Symbol	Example	Pronunciation
x	1. like sh in sheep	**sh**	**peixe**	*paysh*
	2. like s in same	**s**	**próximo**	*praw•see•moo*
	3. like z in lazy	**z**	**exame**	*ee•zuhm*

Letters f, m, p, t and z are pronounced as in English. Letters k, w and y are used only in foreign loan words.

Vowels

Letter	Approximate Pronunciation	Symbol	Example	Pronunciation
a, ã, â	like a in about	**uh**	**anos**	*uh•nooz*
á, à	like a in father	**ah**	**farmácia**	*fuhr•mah•see•uh*
e	1. like e in get	**eh**	**esta**	*eh•stuh*
	2. like ee in eel	**ee**	**exame**	*ee•zuhm*
	3. silent at the end of a word		**leite**	*layt*
	4. occasionally, like i in inn	**i**	**antes**	*ahn•tis*
	5. when combined with the letter i, like ay in say	**ay**	**leite**	*layt*
é	like e in get	**eh**	**esta**	*eh•stuh*
ê	like i in inn	**i**	**mês**	*miz*
i, í	like ee in eel	**ee**	**sim**	*seeng*
o	1. like au in caught	**au**	**onda**	*aun•duh*
	2. at the end of a word, like oo in boo	**oo**	**gato**	*gah•too*
oi	like oy in coy	**oy**	**doi**	*doy*

Letter	Approximate Pronunciation	Symbol	Example	Pronunciation
ó	like aw in paw	**aw**	**história**	*ee•staw•ree•uh*
ô	like u in put	**oah**	**avô**	*uh•voah*
u	1. like oo in boo	**oo**	**uva**	*oo•vuh*
	2. silent after g and q		**guerra**	*geh•rruh*
ú	like oo in boo	**oo**	**úmido**	*oo•mee•thoo*

When a vowel has an accent, you must stress the syllable in the word that contains the accented vowel.

Nasal Sounds

Some nasal sounds are produced when a vowel is followed by the letter **m**. This nasal sound is also found when a combination of certain vowels are used (**ãe**, **ão**, **õe**). These nasal sounds produce either an *ng* sound (e.g., tying) or an *oam* sound (e.g., foam) with the speaker barely pronouncing the g or m.

Letter	Approximate Pronunciation	Symbol	Example	Pronunciation
ãe	like ayin in saying	**eng**	**mãe**	*meng*
ão	like oam in foam	**ohm**	**cão**	*kohm*
õe	like oing in boing	**oing**	**milhões**	*mee•lyoings*
am	at the end of a word, like oam in foam otherwise not nasal: see page 8	**ohm**	**falam**	*fah•loam*
om	like ong in gong	**ohng**	**som**	*sohng*

Letter	Approximate Pronunciation	Symbol	Example	Pronunciation
em	like aying in saying	**eng**	**bem**	*beng*
im	like ing in tying	**ing**	**assim**	*uh•sing*

There are some differences in both the vocabulary and pronunciation of the Portuguese spoken in Portugal and that spoken in Brazil, although people in both countries can easily understand one another. This book is specifically designed for travelers to Brazil.

How to use this Book

Sometimes you see two alternatives separated by a slash. Choose the one that's right for your situation.

ESSENTIAL

Where's the pharmacy [chemist]?	**Onde fica a farmácia?** *aund fee•kuh uh fuhr•mah•see•uh*
What time does the pharmacy open/close?	**A que horas abre/fecha a farmácia?** *uh keh aw•ruhz ah•breh/feh•shuh uh fuhr•mah•see•uh*
What would you recommend for...?	**O que é que me recomenda para...?** *oo keh eh keh meh reh•koo•mehn•duh puh•ruh...*

Words you may see are shown in YOU MAY SEE boxes.

YOU MAY SEE...

CHEGADAS	arrivals
PARTIDAS	departures
ENTREGA DE BAGAGEM	baggage claim

Any of the words or phrases listed can be plugged into the sentence below.

Tickets

When's...	**A que horas é... para...?** *uh kee aw•ruhz eh... puh•ruh*
the (first) bus to	**o (primeiro) ônibus** *uh pree•may•roo) aw•nee•boos*
the (next) flight	**o (próximo) vôo** *oo (praw•see•moo) vau•oo*
the (last) train	**o (último) trem** *oo (ool•tee•moo) treng*

Brazilian Portuguese phrases appear in purple.

Read the simplified pronunciation as if it were English. For more on pronunciation, see page 7.

Conversation

Hello. **Oi.** *au•hee*
How are you? **Tudo bem?** *Too•duh beng*
Fine, thanks. **Bem, obrigado** *m* **/obrigada** *f.* *behm aw•bree•gah•doo/aw•bree•gah•duh*
Excuse me! **Desculpe!** *dehz•kool•peh*

For Numbers, see page 173.

Related phrases can be found by going to the page number indicated.

When different gender forms apply, the masculine form is followed by ***m***; feminine by ***f***

Parking can be difficult in big cities. Always lock your car and never leave anything in sight (even if you consider it not valuable) as it can encourage break-ins.

Information boxes contain relevant country, culture and language tips.

Expressions you may hear are shown in You May Hear boxes.

YOU MAY HEAR...

O que deseja? *oo keh deh•zeh•zsuh* What would you like?
Recomendo... *reh•koo•mehn•doo...* I recommend...
Bom apetite. *bohng uh•peh•tee•teh* Enjoy your meal.

Color-coded side bars identify each section of the book.

Survival

Arrival & Departure

ESSENTIAL

I'm on vacation [holiday]/business.	**Estou de férias/em negócios.** *ee•stawoo deh feh•ree•uhz/eng neh•gaw•see•yooz*
I'm going to…	**Vou para…** *vawoo puh•ruh…*
I'm staying at the… Hotel.	**Estou no hotel…** *ee•stawoo noo aw•tehl…*

YOU MAY HEAR…

O seu bilhete/passaporte. *oo sehoo bee•lyeht /pah•suh•pawrt*	Your ticket/passport, please.
Qual é o propósito de sua visita? *kwahl eh oo prau•paw•zee•too deh soo•uh vee•zee•tuh*	What's the purpose of your visit?
Onde está ficando? *aund ee•stah uh fee•kuhn•doo*	Where are you staying?
Quanto tempo vai ficar? *kwuhn•too tehm•poo veye fee•kahr*	How long are you staying?
Com quem está? *kohm keng ee•stah*	Who are you with?

Border Control

I'm just passing through.	**Estou só de passagem.** *ee•stawoo saw deh puh•sah•zheng*
I would like to declare…	**Queria declarar…** *keh•ree•uh deh•kluh•rahr…*
I have nothing to declare.	**Não tenho nada a declarar.** *nohm teh•nyoo nah•duh uh deh•kluh•rahr*

YOU MAY HEAR...

Tem alguma coisa a declarar? *teng ahl•goo•muh koy•zuh uh deh•kluh•rahr* — Do you have anything to declare?

Tem de pagar direitos [alfandegários] nisto. *teng deh puh•gahr dee•ray•tooz [uhl•fuhn•deh•gah•ree•ooz] nee•stoo* — You must pay duty on this.

Abra esta mala, por favor. *ah•bruh eh•stah mah.lah poor fuh•vaur* — Please open this bag.

YOU MAY SEE...

ALFÂNDEGA	customs
MERCADORIA SEM TAXAS	duty-free goods
ARTIGOS A DECLARAR	goods to declare
NADA A DECLARAR	nothing to declare
CONTROLE DE PASSAPORTES	passport control
POLÍCIA	police

Money

ESSENTIAL

Where's...?	**Onde é...?** *aund eh...*
the ATM	**o caixa eletrônico** *oo keye•shuh uhleh•trau•nee•kau*
the bank	**o banco** *oo buhn•koo*
the currency exchange office	**o câmbio** *oo kuhm•bee•oo*
What time does the bank open/close?	**A que horas o banco abre/fecha?** *uh keh aw•ruhz oo buhn•koo ah•breh/feh•shuh*

I'd like to change dollars/pounds/ euros into reais.	**Queria trocar dólares/libras/euros em reais.** *keh•ree•uh troo•kahr daw•luhrz/lee•bruhz/ ehoo•rooz eng rree•eyez*
I want to cash some traveler's checks [cheques].	**Quero trocar cheques de viagem.** *keh•roo troo•kahr sheh•kehz deh vee•ah•zseng*

At the Bank

Can I exchange foreign currency/get a cash advance here?	**Posso trocar moedas estrangeiras/ obter dinheiro a crédito aqui?** *paw•soo troo•kahr moo•eh•duhz ee•struhn•zsay•ruhz au•btehr dee•nyay•roo uh kreh•dee•too uh•kee*
What's the exchange rate?	**Quanto está o câmbio?** *kwuhn•too ee•stah oo kuhm•bee•oo*
How much commission do you charge?	**Quanto cobram de comissão?** *kwuhn•too kaw•brohm deh koo•mee•sohm*
I think there's a mistake.	**Penso que há um erro.** *pehn•soo keh ah oong eh•rroo*
I've lost my traveler's checks [cheques].	**Perdio meu talão de cheques.** *pehr•dee oo mehoo tah.lohm deh sheh•kehz*
My card was lost.	**O meu cartão foi perdido.** *oo mehoo kuhr•tohm foy pehr•dee•thoo*
My credit card has been stolen.	**Roubaram o meu cartão de crédito.** *raw•bah•rohm oo mehoo kuhr•tohm deh kreh•dee•too*
My credit card doesn't work.	**O meu cartão de crédito não funciona.** *oo mehoo kuhr•tohm deh kreh•dee•too nohm foon•see•au•nuh*
The ATM ate my card.	**O caixa eletrônico ficou com o meu cartão.** *uh cah•ee•shah uh•leh•trau•nee•kau fee•kawoo kaum oo mehoo kuhr•tohm*

For Numbers, see page 173.

YOU MAY SEE…

INSERIR O CARTÃO	insert card here
CANCELAR	cancel
APAGAR	clear
CONFIRMAR	enter
PIN	PIN
RETIRAR DINHEIRO	withdraw funds
DA CONTA CORRENTE	from checking [current] account
DA CONTA DE POUPANÇA	from savings account
RECIBO	receipt

Currency exchange offices (**Câmbio**) can be found in most Brazilian tourist centers; they generally stay open longer than banks, especially during the summer season. Travel agencies and hotels are other places where you can exchange money, but the rate will not be as good. In heavy tourist areas, you can also find currency exchange machines/ATMs on the streets. Of course, you should use caution when exchanging/withdrawing money on the street, especially in cities where crime rates are high. Remember to take your passport with you when you want to change money.

YOU MAY SEE…

The currency in Brazil is the **real (R$)**, plural **reais**, divided into 100 **centavos**.
Coins: 1, 5, 10, 25, 50 **centavos**; 1 **R$**
Notes: 2, 5, 10, 20, 50, 100 **R$**

Getting Around

ESSENTIAL

How do I get to the city center?	**Como vou para o centro da cidade?** *kau•moo vawoo puh•ruh oo sehn•troo duh see•dahd*
Where's...?	**Onde é...?** *aund eh...*
the airport	**o aeroporto** *oo uh•eh•rau•paur•too*
the train station	**a estação ferroviária** *uh ee•stuh•sohm feh•rroo•vee•ah•ree•uh*
the bus station	**a estação de ônibus** *uh ee•stuh•sohm deh aw•nee•boos*
the metro [underground] station	**a estação de metrô** *uh ee•stuh•sohm deh meh•troo*
How far is it?	**A que distância fica?** *uh keh dee•stuhn•see•uh fee•kuh*
Where can I buy tickets?	**Onde posso comprar bilhetes?** *aund paw•soo kaum•prahr bee•lyehtz*
A one-way/return-trip ticket to...	**Um bilhete de ida/de ida e volta para...** *oong bee•lyeht deh ee•thuh/deh ee•thuh ee vaul•tuh puh•ruh...*
How much?	**Quanto custa?** *kwuhn•too koo•stuh*
Are there any discounts?	**Há descontos?** *ah dehs•caun•tooz*
Which...?	**Qual...?** *kwahl...*
gate	**porta** *port•uh*
line	**linha** *lee•nyuh*
platform	**plataforma** *plah•tuh•fawr•muh*
Where can I get a taxi?	**Onde posso pegar um táxi?** *aund paw•soo peh•gahr oong tahk•see*

Please take me to this address.	**Leve-me neste endereço.** *leh•veh•meh nehst ehn•deh•reh•soo*
Where can I rent a car?	**Onde posso alugar um carro?** *aund paw•soo uh•loo•gahr oong kah•rroo*
Could I have a map?	**Pode me dar um mapa?** *pawd meh dahr oong mah•puh*

Tickets

When's...to...?	**A que horas é...para...?** *uh kee aw•ruhz eh... puh•ruh...*
the (first) bus	**o (primeiro) ônibus** *uh (pree•may•ruh) aw•nee•boos*
the (next) flight	**o (próximo) vôo** *oo (praw•see•moo) vau•oo*
the (last) train	**o (último) trem** *oo (ool•tee•moo) treng*
Where can I buy tickets?	**Onde posso comprar bilhetes?** *aund paw•soo kaum•prahr bee•lyehtz*
One/Two ticket(s), please.	**Um bilhete/Dois bilhetes, por favor.** *oong bee•lyeht/doyz bee•lyehtz poor fuh•vaur*
For today/tomorrow.	**Para hoje/amanhã.** *puh•ruh auzseh/uh•muh•nyuh*
A...ticket.	**Um bilhete...** *oong bee•lyeht...*
one-way	**de ida** *deh ee•thuh*
return-trip	**de ida e volta** *deh ee•thuh ee vaul•tuh*
first-class	**em primeira classe** *eng pree•may•ruh klah•she* *business class*
economy class	**em classe econômica** *eng klah•seh eh•koo•naw•mee•kuh*
How much?	**Quanto custa?** *kwuhn•too koo•stuh*
Is there a discount for...?	**Há desconto para...?** *ah dehs•kaum•too puh•ruh...*
children	**crianças** *kree•uhn•suhz*
students	**estudantes** *ee•stoo•duhnts*
senior citizens	**idosos** *ee•daw•zooz*

tourists	**turistas** *too•ree•stuhz*
The express bus/express train, please.	**A ônibus expresso/o trem expresso, por favor.** *uh aw•nee•boos /oo treng ees•preh•soo, poor fuh•vaur*
The local bus/train, please.	**A ônibus/o trem local, por favor.** *uh aw•nee•boos /oo treng loo•kahl, poor fuh•vaur*
I have an e-ticket.	**Eu tenho um bilhete electrônico.** *ehoo teh•nyoo oong bee•lyeht ee•le•tro•nee•kuh*
Can I buy a ticket on the bus/train?	**Posso comprar o bilhete no ônibus/no trem?** *paw•soo kaum•prahr oo bee•lyeht noo aw•nee•boos/noo treng*
Do I have to stamp the ticket before boarding?	**Tenho de carimbar o bilhete antes de embarcar?** *teh•nyoo deh kuh•reem•bahr oo bee•lyeht uhnts deh ehm•buhr•kahr*
How long is this ticket valid?	**Até quando este bilhete é válido?** *uh•teh kwuhn doo ehst bee•lyeht eh vah•lee•doo*
Can I return on the same ticket?	**Posso voltar com o mesmo bilhete?** *paw•soo vaul•tuhr kaum oo mehz•moo bee•lyeht*
I'd like to. . .my reservation.	**Queria. . .a minha reserva.** *keh•ree•uh. . .uh mee•nyuh reh•zehr•vuh*
cancel	**cancelar** *kuhn•seh•lahr*
change	**mudar** *moo•dahr*
confirm	**confirmar** *kaum•feer•mahr*

Plane

Airport Transfer

How much is a taxi to the airport? **Quanto custa um táxi para o aeroporto?** *kwuhn•too koo•stuh oong tahk•see puh•ruh oo uh•eh•rau•paur•too*

To...Airport, please. **Ao aeroporto de..., por favor.** *ahoo uh•eh•rau•paur•too deh...poor fuh•vaur*

My airline is... **A minha linha aérea é...** *uh mee•nyuh lee•nyuh ah•ehr•ee•uh eh...*

My flight leaves at... **O meu vôo parte às...** *oo meeoo vau•oo pahr•teh ahz...*

I'm in a hurry. **Estou com pressa.** *ee•stawoo kaum preh•suh*

Can you take an alternate route? **Pode tomar um caminho alternativo?** *pawd too•mahr oong kuh•mee•nyoo ahl•tehr•nah•tee•vuh*

Can you drive faster/slower? **Pode dirigir mais rápido/devagar?** *pawd dee·ree·jeer meyez rah•pee•thoo/deh•vuh•gahr*

For Time, see page 175.

YOU MAY SEE...

CHEGADAS	arrivals
PARTIDAS	departures
ENTREGA DE BAGAGEM	baggage claim
VÔOS DOMÉSTICOS	domestic flights
VÔOS INTERNACIONAIS	international flights
BALCÃO DE CHECK-IN	check-in desk
REGISTRO DE BILHETE ELECTRÔNICO	e-ticket check-in
PORTÕES DE PARTIDA	departure gates

YOU MAY HEAR...

Que linha aérea voam? *keh lee•nyuh ah•eh•ree•uh vau•ohm*	What airline are you flying?
Doméstico ou internacional? *thoo•meh•stee•koo awoo een•tehr•nuh•seeoo•nahl*	Domestic or international?
Que terminal? *keh tehr•mee•nahl*	What terminal?

Checking In

Where is the check-in counter?	**Onde é o check in?** *aund eh oo check in*
My name is...	**Meu nome é...** *mehoo nau•mee eh...*
I'm going to...	**Vou para...** *vauoo puh•ruh...*
I have...	**Tenho...** *teh•nyoo...*
one suitcase	**uma mala** *oo•muh mah•luh*
two suitcases	**duas malas** *thoo•uhz mah•luhs*
one piece of hand luggage	**uma bagagem de mão** *oo•muh buh•gah•zsen deh mohm*

How much luggage is allowed?	**Quantas bagagens são permitidas?** *kwuhn•tuhz buh•gah•zsengs sohm pehr•mee•tee•thuhs*
Is that pounds or kilos?	**Isso está em libras ou quilos?** *ee•soo ee•stah eng lee•bruhz awoo kee•laes*
Which terminal/gate does flight...leave from?	**Qual é o terminal para o vôo/a porta do vôo para...?** *kwahl eh oo tehr•mee•nahl puh•ruh oo vau•oo/uh pawr•tuhz thoo vau•oo puh•ruh...*
I'd like a window/ an aisle seat.	**Queria um lugar na janela/no corredor.** *keh•ree•uh oong loo•gahr nah zsuh•neh•luh/ noo koo•rreh•daur*
When do we leave/ arrive?	**Quando vamos partir/chegar?** *kwuhn•doo vuh•mooz puhr•teer/shee•gahr*
Is flight...delayed?	**Há atraso no vôo...?** *ah uh•trah•zoo noo vau•oo...*
How late will it be?	**Qual é o atraso?** *kwahl eh oo uh•trah•zoo*

Luggage

Where is/are...?	**Onde é/são...?** *aund eh/sohm...*
the luggage trolleys	**os carrinhos** *ooz kuh•rree•nyos*
the luggage lockers	**os armários de bagagem** *ooz ahr•mah•ree•uhz deh buh•gah•zseng*
the baggage claim	**o depósito de bagagem** *oo deh•paw•zee•too deh buh•gah•zseng*
My luggage has been lost.	**Perdi a minha bagagem.** *pehr•dee uh mee•nyuh buh•gah•zseng*
My luggage has been stolen.	**Roubaram a minha bagagem.** *raw•bah•rohm uh mee•nyuh buh•gah•zseng*
My suitcase was damaged.	**A minha mala foi danificada.** *uh mee•nyuh mah•luh foy deh•nee•fee•kah•thuh*

YOU MAY HEAR...

Próximo! *praw•see•moo* — Next!

O seu bilhete/passaporte, por favor. *oo sehoo bee•lyet/pah•suh•pawrt poor fuh•vaur* — Your ticket/passport, please.

Tem bagagem para despachar? *teng buh•gah•zseng puh•ruh dehs•puh•shahr* — Are you checking any luggage?

Tem excesso de peso na sua bagagem. *teng eh•zeh•soo deh peh•zoo nuh soo•uh buh•gah•zseng* — You have excess baggage.

Isso é muito volumoso para bagagem de mão. *ee•soo eh moo.ee.too vaw•loo•mau•zoo puh•ruh buh•gah•zseng deh mohm* — That's too large for a carry-on [to carry on board].

Foi o senhor *m* **/a senhora** *f* **quem fez as malas?** *foy oo see•nyaur/ uh see•nyau•ruh keng fehz uhs mah•luhs* — Did you pack these bags yourself?

Alguém lhe deu alguma coisa para transportar? *ahl•geng lyeh dehoo ahl•goo•muh coy•zuh puh•ruh truhns•pawr•tahr* — Did anyone give you anything to carry?

Tire tudo dos bolsos. *tee•reh too•thoo dooz bawl•sooz* — Empty your pockets.

Tire os seus sapatos. *tee•reh ooz sehooz suh•pah•tooz* — Take off your shoes.

Estamos a embarcar o vôo... *ee•stuh•mooz uh eng•buhr•kahr oo vau•oo...* — Now boarding flight...

Finding your Way

Where is/are…?	**Onde é/são…?** *aund eh/sohm*
the currency exchange office	**o câmbio** *oo kuhm•bee•oo*
the car hire	**o aluguel de carros** *oo uh•loo•gehl deh kah•rrooz*
the exit	**a saída** *uh suh•ee•thuh*
the taxis	**os táxis** *ooz tahk•seez*
Is there…into town?	**Há…para o centro?** *ah…puh•ruh oo sehn•troo*
a bus	**um ônibus** *oong aw•nee•boos*
a train	**um trem** *oong treng*
a metro [underground]	**um metrô** *oong meh•troo*

For Asking Directions, see page 36.

Train

Where's the nearest train station?	**Onde está a estação de trens mais próxima?** *aund ee•stah uh ee•stuh•sohm deh trengs meyez praw•see•muh*
How far is it?	**A que distância fica?** *uh keh dee•stuhn•see•uh fee•kuh*

Where is/are...?	**Onde está/são...?** *aund ee•stah/sohm...*
the ticket office	**a bilheteria** *uh bee•lyeht•eh•ree•uh*
the information desk	**as informações** *uhz een•foor•muh•soingz*
the luggage lockers	**os armários de bagagem** *ooz ahr•mah•ree•uhz deh buh•gah•zseng*
the platforms	**as plataformas** *uhz plah•tuh•fawr•muhz*
Could I have a schedule [timetable], please?	**Queria um horário, por favor.** *keh•ree•uh oong aw•rah•ree•oo poor fuh•vaur*
How long is the trip?	**Quanto tempo demora a viagem?** *kwuhn•too tehm•poo deh•maw•ruh uh vee•ah•zseng*
Is it a direct train?	**É um trem directo?** *eh oong treng dee•reh•too*
Do I have to change trains?	**Tenho de mudar de trem?** *teh•nyoo deh moo•dahr deh treng*
Is the train on time?	**O trem chega a horas?** *oo treng shee•gah uh aw•ruhz*

For Tickets, see page 20.

Departures

Which track [platform] for the train to...?	**De que plataforma parte o trem para...?** *deh keh plah•tuh•fawr•muh pahrt oo treng puh•ruh...*
Is this the track [platform] to...?	**É daqui que parte o trem para...?** *eh duh•kee keh pahrt oo treng puh•ruh...*
Where is track [platform]...?	**Onde é a plataforma...?** *aund eh uh plah•tuh•fawr•muh...*
Where do I change for...?	**Onde é que mudo para...?** *aund eh keh moo•thoo puh•ruh...*

On Board

Is this seat taken?	**Este lugar está ocupado?** *ehst loo•gahr ee•stah aw•koo•pah•thoo*
Can I sit here/ open the window?	**Posso sentar aqui/abrir a janela?** *paw•soo sehn•tahr uh•kee/ah•breer uh zsuh•neh•luh*
That's my seat.	**Esse é o meu lugar.** *eh•seh eh oo mehoo loo•gahr*
Here's my reservation.	**Aqui está a minha reserva.** *uh•kee ee•stah uh mee•nyuh reh•zehr•vuh*

YOU MAY SEE...

PARA AS LINHAS	to the platforms
INFORMAÇÕES	information
RESERVAS	reservations
SALA DE ESPERA	waiting room
CHEGADAS	arrivals
PARTIDAS	departures

In Brazil the rail network is quite small. The Brazilian railway, **Estrada de Ferro Central do Brasil (E.F.C.B.)**, offers few passenger services. The São Paulo–Rio de Janeiro night journey is comfortable but long and expensive.

Bus

Where's the bus station?	**Onde é a estação de ônibus?** *aund eh uh ee•stuh•sohm deh áw•nee•boos*
How far is it?	**A que distância fica?** *uh keh dee•stuhn•see•uh fee•kuh*
How do I get to…?	**Como se vai para…?** *kau•moo seh veye puh•ruh…*
Does the bus [coach] stop at…?	**O ônibus pára em…?** *uh oo aw•nee•boos pah•ruh eng…*
Could you tell me when to get off?	**Pode-me dizer quando devo sair?** *paw•deh meh dee•zehr kwuhn•doo deh•voo suh•eer*

YOU MAY HEAR…

Todos a bordo! *toah•thooz uh baur•thoo*	All aboard!
Bilhetes, por favor. *bee•lyehtz poor fuh•vaur*	Tickets, please.
Tem de mudar em… *teng deh moo•dahr eng…*	You have to change at…
A próxima parada… *uh praw•see•muh puh•rah•duh…*	Next stop…

Do I have to change buses?	**Tenho de mudar de autocarro [ônibus]?** *teh•nyoo deh moo•dahr deh ahoo•too•kah•rroo [aw•nee•boos]*
Stop here, please!	**Pare aqui, por favor!** *pah•reh uh•kee poor fuh•vaur*

For Tickets, see page 20.

Intercity buses are fairly cheap and comfortable, usually with air conditioning. If you are traveling overnight, look for **leitos**, buses with reclining seats, clean sheets and pillows. Tickets are available from bus stations (**rodoviárias**).

Metro

Where's the nearest metro [underground] station?	**Onde é a estação de metrô mais próxima?** *aund eh uh ee•stuh•sohm deh meh•troo meyez praw•see•muh*
Could I have a map of the subway [underground], please?	**Pode me dar um mapa do metrô, por favor?** *pawd meh dahr oong mah•puh thoo meh•troo poor fuh•vaur*
Which line for...?	**Qual é a linha para...?** *kwahl eh uh lee•nyuh puh•ruh...*
Do I have to transfer [change]?	**Tenho que mudar?** *teh•nyoo keh moo•dahr*
Is this the metro to...?	**Este trem vai para...?** *ehst treng veye puh•ruh...*
Where are we?	**Onde estamos?** *aund ee•stuh•mooz*

For Tickets, see page 20.

São Paulo, Rio de Janeiro, Belo Horizonte, Porto Alegre and Recife have excellent modern metro systems, though not covering the whole city. Tickets available are: **unitário** (one-way), **múltiplo 2** (round-trip), **múltiplo 10** (ten trips) and **integração** (one metro + one bus).

Boat & Ferry

When is the ferry to…?	**Quando é a balsa para…?** *kwuhn•doo eh uh bahl•suh puh•ruh…*
Can I take my car?	**Posso levar o meu carro?** *paw•soo loo•vahr oo mehoo kah•rroo*
What time is the next sailing?	**A que horas parte o próximo barco?** *au qeh aw•ruhz pahr•teh oo praw•see•moo bahr•koo*
Can I book a seat/cabin?	**Posso reservar um lugar/uma cabine?** *paw•soo reh•zehr•vuhr oong loo•gahr/oo•muh kuh•bee•nuh*
How long is the crossing?	**Quanto tempo demora a viagem?** *kwuhn•too tehm•poo deh•maw•ruh uh vee•ah•zseng*

There are specially organized cruises in all coastal towns in Brazil for visits to main beaches and nearby islands.Transport between Belém, Manaus and Santarém can be done by boat across the Amazon River, departing from **hidroviárias** (ferry terminals); for the long night journey, a hammock on deck is preferable to a hot cabin. Cruises on the Amazon are run by the state-owned **Empresa de Navegação da Amazônia (E.N.A.S.A.)** and a number of private companies.

YOU MAY SEE...

BARCO SALVA-VIDAS	life boat
COLETE SALVA-VIDAS	life jacket

Taxi

Where can I get a taxi?	**Onde posso pegar um táxi?** *aund paw•soo peh•gahr oong tahk•see*
Can you send a taxi?	**Pode enviar um táxi?** *pawd ehn•vee•ahr oong tahk•see*

I'd like a taxi now/ for tomorrow at...	**Queria um táxi agora/amanhã às...** *keh•ree•uh oong tahk•see uh•gaw•ruh/uh•muh•nyuh ahz...*
Pick me up at... (place/time)	**Me pegue no/às...** *meh peh•geh noo/ahz...*
I'm going to...	**Vou para...** *vau•oo puh•ruh...*
this address	**este endereço** *ehst ehn•deh•reh•soo*
the airport	**o aeroporto** *oo uh•eh•rau•paur•too*
the train [railway] station	**à estação dee trem** *ah ee•stuh•sohm deh treng*
I'm late.	**Estou atrasado** *m* **/atrasada** *f*. *ee•stawoo uh•truh•zah•thoo/uh•truh•zah•thuh*
Can you drive faster/ slower?	**Pode dirigir mais rápido/devagar?** *pawd dee•ree•jeer meyez rrah•pee•thoo/deh•vuh•gahr*
Stop/Wait here.	**Pare/Espere aqui.** *pah•reh/ee•speh•reh uh•kee*
How much?	**Quanto é?** *kwuhn•too eh*
You said it would cost...reais.	**Disse que ia custar...reais.** *thee•seh keh ee•uh koo•stahr...rree•eyez*
A receipt, please.	**Um recibo, por favor.** *oong reh•see•boo por fahz fuh•vaur*
Keep the change.	**Guarde o troco.** *goo•ahr•deh oo trau•koo*

YOU MAY HEAR...

Para onde? *puh•ruh aun•deh*	Where to?
Qual é o endereço? *kwahl eh uh ehn•deh•reh•soo*	What's the address?
Há uma taxa extra noturna/de aeroporto. *ah oo•muh tah•shuh ehs•truh naw•toor•nuh/ deh uh•eh•rau•paur•too*	There's a nighttime/ airport surcharge.

Taxis are yellow in Rio de Janeiro and white in São Paulo. Fares are generally cheap. All Brazilian taxis have meters, except in small towns, where the fare should be agreed in advance. R$ 0.20–0.90 is an approriate tip.

Bicycle & Motorbike

Where can I rent…? **Onde posso alugar…?** *aund paw•soo uh•loo•gahr…*

a 3-/10-speed bicycle **uma bicicleta de trêz/dez velocidades [marchas]** *oo•muh bee•see•kleh•tuh deh trehz/dehz veh•law•see•dah•dehz [mahr•shuhz]*

a moped **uma lambreta** *oo•muh luhm•breh•tuh*

a motorcycle **uma motocicleta** *oo•muh maw•taw•see•kleh•tuh*

How much per day/ week? **Quanto custa por dia/semana?** *kwuhn•too koo•stuh poor dee•uh/seh•muh•nuh*

Can I have a helmet/ lock? **Posso ter uma capacete/corrente?** *paw•soo tehr oo•muh kuh•puh•seh•the/koo•rrehnt*

Car Hire

Where can I rent a car? **Onde posso alugar um carro?** *aund paw•soo uh•loo•gahr oong kah•rroo*

I'd like to rent… **Queria alugar…** *keh•ree•uh uh•loo•gahr…*

a cheap/small car **um carro barato/pequeno** *oong kah•rroo buh•rah•too/peh•keh•noo*

a 2-/4-door car **um carro de duas/quatro portas** *oong kah•rroo deh thoo•uhz/kwah•troo pawr•tuhz*

a(n) automatic/ manual **um carro automático/manual** *oong kah•rroo awoo•too•mah•tee•koo/mah.noo.ahl*

a car with air conditioning **um carro com ar condicionado** *oong kah•rroo kaum ahr kawn•dee•seeoo•nah•thoo*

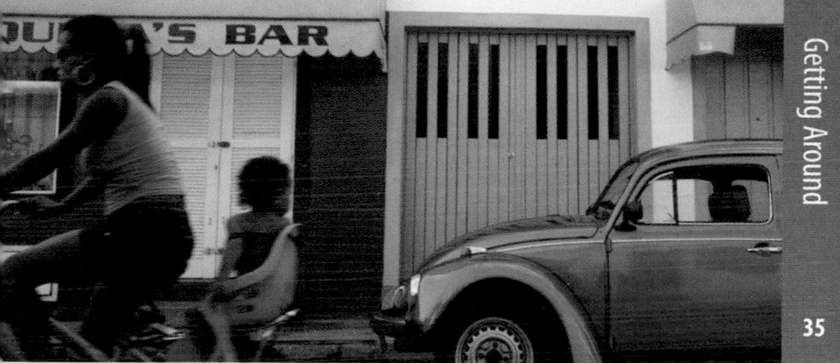

a car seat	**um assento de carro de bebê** *oong uh•sehn•too deh kah•rroo deh beh•beh*
How much...	**Quanto é...?** *kwuhn•too eh...*
per day/week	**por dia/semana** *poor dee•uh/seh•muh•nuh*
per kilometer	**por quilômetro** *poor kee•law•meh•troo*
for unlimited mileage	**com quilometragem ilimitada** *kaum kee•lae•meh•trah•zseng ee•lee•mee•tah•thuh*
with insurance	**com seguro** *kaum seh•goo•roo*
Are there any discounts?	**Há descontos?** *ah dehs•kaum•tooz*

Fuel Station

Where's the next fuel station?	**Onde é o posto mais próximo?** *aund eh oo paws•too meyez praw•see•moo*
Fill it up, please.	**Encha o tanque, por favor.** *ehn•shuh oo tuhn•keh poor fuh•vaur*
...liters, please.	**...litros, por favor.** *...lee•trooz poor fuh•vaur*
I'll pay in cash/by credit card.	**Pago com dinheiro/com o cartão de crédito.** *pah•goo kaum dee•nyay•roo/kaum oo kuhr•tohm deh kreh•dee•too*

YOU MAY HEAR...

Tem uma carta de condução internacional? *teng oo•muh kahr•tuh deh kaum•doo•sohm een•tehr•nuh•see•oo•nahl*	Do you have an international driver's license?
O seu passaporte, por favor. *oo sehoo pah•suh•pawr•teh poor fuh•vaur*	Your passport, please.
Quer seguro? *kehr seh•goo•roo*	Do you want insurance?
É preciso deixar um sinal de... *eh preh•see•zoo day•shahr oong see•nahl deh...*	There is a deposit of...
Assine aqui, por favor. *uh•see•neh uh•kee poor fuh•vaur*	Please sign here.

YOU MAY SEE...

NORMAL	regular
SUPER	premium [super]
DIESEL	diesel

Asking Directions

Is this the right road to...?	**Esta é a estrada que vai para...?** *eh•stuh eh uh ee•strah•duh keh veye puh•ruh...*
How far is it to...?	**A que distância fica...?** *uh keh dee•stuhn•see•uh fee•kuh...*
Where's...?	**Onde fica...?** *aund fee•kuh...*
...Street	**a rua...** *uh rroo•uh...*
this address	**neste endereço** *nehst ehn•deh•reh•soo*
the highway [motorway]	**a estrada** *uh strah•duh*

Can you show me on the map?	**Pode indicar no mapa?** *pawd een•dee•kahr noo mah•puh*
I'm lost.	**Estou perdido** ***m*** **/perdida** ***f*****.** *ee•stawoo pehr•dee•doo/pehr•dee•duh*

Parking

Can I park here?	**Posso estacionar aqui?** *paw•soo ee•stuh•seeoo•nahr uh•kee*
Where is the nearest parking garage/ parking lot [car park]?	**Onde fica a garagem mais próxima/o estacionamento mais próximo?** *aund fee•kuh uh guh•rah•zseng meyez praw•see•muh/ oo ee•stuh•seeawn•uh•mehn•too meyez praw•see•moo*
Where's the parking meter?	**Onde está o parquímetro?** *aund ee•stah oo pahr•kee•meh•troo*

YOU MAY HEAR...

sempre em frente *sehm•preh eng frehn•teh*	straight ahead
à esquerda *ah ee•skehr•duh*	on the left
à direita *ah dee•ray•tuh*	on the right
depois da/ao dobrar a esquina *deh•poyz dah/ahoo doo•brahr uh ees•kee•nuh*	on/around the corner
em frente de *eng frehn•teh deh*	opposite
por trás de *poor trahz deh*	behind
a seguir ao ***m*** **/à** ***f*** *uh seh•geer ahoo/ah*	next to
depois do ***m*** **/da** ***f*** *deh•poyz thoo/duh*	after
norte/sul *nawrt/sool*	north/south
leste/oeste *lehs•the/aw•ehs•teh*	east/west
no semáforo *noo seh•mah•fau•roo*	at the traffic light
no cruzamento *noo croo•zuh•mehn•too*	at the intersection

YOU MAY SEE...

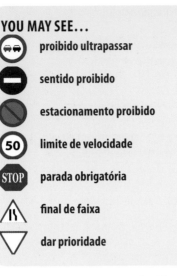

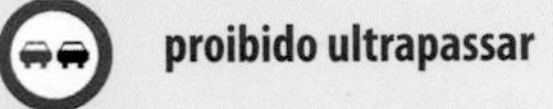	**proibido ultrapassar**	do not pass
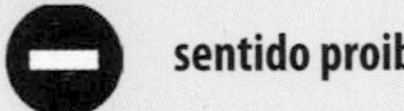	**sentido proibido**	no entry
	**estacionamento proibido**	no parking
	**limite de velocidade**	speed limit
	**parada obrigatória**	stop
	**final de faixa**	lane ends
	**dar prioridade**	yield

How much? **Quanto é...?** *kwuhn•too eh...*
  per hour **por hora** *poor aw•ruh*
  per day **por dia** *poor dee•uh*
  overnight **só uma noite** *saw oo•muh noyt*

Parking can be difficult in big cities. Always lock your car and never leave anything in sight (even if you consider it not valuable) as it can encourage break-ins. Parking "guards" tend to appear within seconds of parking your car, offering to watch over it for you for a (modest) fee. It is advisable to agree to this as otherwise you may risk returning to a slightly damaged vehicle. Licensed guards operate in Rio and São Paulo. They will issue a receipt that covers a set period of time.

Rio drivers are especially notorious for their erratic lane-changing, in-town speeding and disregard for pedestrians and other drivers on the road. Be on the defensive and expect the unexpected. Speeding fines can be huge (several hundred dollars) even if going only slightly over the limit, which can change erratically. Be warned, it is polite to beep your horn when overtaking, and flashing your lights as a warning is common. It is illegal to drink and drive and there is a zero tolerance policy in operation. If in doubt, take a cab.

Breakdown & Repair

My car broke down/ won't start.	**O meu carro quebrou/O motor não pega.** *oo mehoo kah•rroo keh•brawoo/oo moo•taur nohm peh•guh*
Can you fix it (today)?	**Pode consertá-lo (hoje)?** *pawd kaum•sehr•tah•loo (oyzseh)*
When will it be ready?	**Quando estará pronto?** *kwuhn•doo ee•stuh•rah praun•too*
How much is it?	**Quanto custa?** *kwuhn•too koo•stuh*
I have a puncture/flat tyre (tire).	**Tenho um furo/pneu sem ar.** *teh•nyoo oong foo•roo/pnehoo seng ahr*

Accidents

There has been an accident.	**Houve um acidente.** *auoov oong uh•see•dehnt*
Call an ambulance/ the police.	**Chame uma ambulância/a polícia.** *shuh•meh oo•muh uhm•boo•luhn•see•uh/uh poo•lee•see•uh*

Places to Stay

ESSENTIAL

Can you recommend a hotel?	**Pode recomendar um hotel?** *pawd reh•kaw•mehn•dahr oong aw•tehl*
I have a reservation.	**Tenho uma reserva.** *teh•nyoo oo•muh reh•zehr•vuh*
My name is...	**Meu nome é...** *mehoo naum•eh eh...*
Do you have a room...?	**Tem um quarto...?** *teng oong kwahr•too...*
for one/two	**para um/dois** *puh•ruh oong/doyz*
with a bathroom	**com banheiro** *kaum buh•nyay•roo*
with air conditioning	**com ar condicionado** *kaum ar kawn•dee•seeoo•nah•thoo*
For...	**Para...** *puh•ruh...*
tonight	**hoje à noite** *auzseh ah noyt*
two nights	**duas noites** *thoo•uhz noytz*
one week	**uma semana** *oo•muh seh•muh•nuh*
How much is it?	**Quanto custa?** *kwuhn•too koo•stuh*
Do you have anything cheaper?	**Há mais barato?** *ah meyez buh•rah•too*
What time is check-out?	**A que horas temos de deixar o quarto?** *uh kee aw•ruhz teh•mooz deh thay•shahr oo kwahr•too*
Can I leave this in the safe?	**Posso deixar isto no cofre?** *paw•soo thay•shahr ee•stoo noo kaw•freh*
Can I leave my bags?	**Posso deixar a minha bagagem?** *paw•soo day•shahr uh mee•nyuh buh•gah•geng*
Can I have the bill/a receipt?	**Pode me dar a conta/um recibo?** *pawd meh dahr uh kaum•tuh/oong reh•see•boo*
I'll pay in cash/by credit card.	**Pago com dinheiro/com o cartão de crédito.** *pah•goo kaum dee•nyay•roo/kaum oo kuhr•tohm deh kreh•dee•too*

Somewhere to Stay

Can you recommend…? **Pode recomendar…?** *pawd reh•kaw•mehn•dahr*

a hotel **um hotel** *oong aw•tehl*

a hostel **um albergue** *oong ahl•behrg*

a campsite **um parque de campismo** *oong pahr•keh deh kuhm•peez•moo*

a bed and breakfast **uma pousada** *oo•muh pawoo•zah•thuh*

What is it near? **É perto de quê?** *eh pehr•too deh keh*

How do I get there? **Como se vai para lá?** *kau•moo seh veye puh•ruh lah*

At the Hotel

I have a reservation. **Tenho uma reserva.** *teh•nyoo oo•muh reh•zehr•vuh*

My name is… **Meu nome é…** *mehoo naum•ee eh…*

Do you have a room…? **Tem um quarto…?** *teng oong kwahr•too…*

with a bathroom [toilet]/shower **com banheiro/chuveiro** *kaum buh•nyay•roo/shoo•vay•roo*

with air conditioning **com ar condicionado** *kaum ar kawn•dee•seeoo•nah•thoo*

that's smoking/non-smoking **para fumantes/não-fumantes** *puh•ruh foo•muhnts/nohm-foo•muhnts*

For...	**Para...** *puh•ruh...*
tonight	**hoje à noite** *auzseh ah noyt*
two nights	**duas noites** *thoo•uhz noytz*
one week	**uma semana** *oo•muh seh•muh•nuh*
Does the hotel have...?	**O hotel tem...?** *oo aw•tehl teng...*
a computer	**um computador** *oong kaum•poo•tuh•daur*
an elevator [lift]	**um elevador** *oong eh•leh•vuh•daur*
(wireless) internet service	**serviço de internet (sem fios)** *sehr•vee•soo deh een•tehr•neht (seng fee•ooz)*
room service	**serviço de quartos** *sehr•vee•soo deh kwahr•tooz*
a pool	**piscina** *pee•see•nuh*
a gym	**uma academia** *oo•muh ah•kah•duh•mee•ah*
I need...	**Preciso de...** *preh•see•zoo deh...*
an extra bed	**outra cama** *auoo•truh kuh•muh*
a cot	**cama de lona** *kuh•muh deh law•nuh*
a crib	**uma cama de bebê** *oo•muh kuh•muh de beh•beh*

For Numbers, see page 173.

In Brazil, the cheapest place to stay is the **dormitório**, providing a shared room for a few **reais** per night. Other kinds of lodging include:

Hotel In Brazil, most hotels are regulated by **Embratur** (the Brazilian Tourism Authority). There are five official categories.

Hotel-Apartamento Apartment hotels ranging from 2- to 4-star.

Hotel fazenda Farmhouse lodges, generally equipped with a swimming pool, tennis court and horseback-riding facilities.

Pousada A state-owned inn converted from an old castle, monastery, convent, palace or in a location of interest to tourists.

Pensão Corresponds to a boarding house. Usually divided into four categories.

Pousada de juventude Youth hostel; there are over 90 youth hostels in Brazil, which are open to anyone, regardless of age, though members can obtain discounts. Hostels are extremely popular and the best ones book up quickly so it is best to book these in advance.

Residencial Bed and breakfast accommodations.

Price

How much per night/ week?	**Quanto é por noite/semana?** *kwuhn•too eh poor noyt/seh•muh•nuh*
Does the price include breakfast/sales tax?	**O preço inclui o café da manhã/taxas?** *oo preh•soo een•kloo•ee oo kuh•feh duh muh•nyuh/ tah•shuhz*
Are there any discounts?	**Há algum desconto?** *ah ahl•goong dehs•kaum•too*

YOU MAY HEAR...

O seu passaporte/cartão de crédito, por favor. *oo sehoo pah•suh•pawrt/kuhr•tohm deh kreh•dee•too poor fuh•vaur*	Your passport/credit card, please.
Preencha esta ficha, por favor. *pree•ehn•shuh eh•stuh fee•shuh poor fuh•vaur*	Please fill out this form.
Assine aqui. *uh•see•neh uh•kee*	Sign here.

Preferences

Can I see the room?	**Posso ver o quarto?** *paw•soo vehr oo kwahr•too*
I'd like a...room.	**Queria um... quarto.** *keh•ree•uh oong...kwahr•too*
better	**melhor** *meh•lyohr*
bigger	**maior** *muh•eeohr*
cheaper	**mais barato** *meyez buh•rah•too*
quieter	**mais silencioso** *meyez see•lehn•see•aw•zoo*
I'll take it.	**Fico com esse.** *fee•koo kaum eh•seh.*
No, I won't take it.	**Não, não fico com esse.** *nohm, nohm fee•koo kaum eh•seh*

Questions

Where's...?	**Onde é...?** *aund eh...*
the bar	**o bar** *oo bar*
the bathroom [toilet]	**a casa de banho [o banheiro]** *uh kah•zuh deh buh•nyoo [oo buh•nyay•roo]*
the elevator [lift]	**o elevador** *oo eh•leh•vuh•daur*
Can I have...?	**Queria um...** *keh•ree•uh oong...*
a blanket	**um cobertor** *oong koo•behr•taur*
an iron	**um ferro** *oong feh•rroo*
a pillow	**um travesseiro** *oong truh•veh•say•roo*

soap	**um sabonete** *oong suh•boo•neht*
toilet paper	**papel higiênico** *puh•pehl ee•zseh•nee•koo*
a towel	**uma toalha** *oo•muh too•ah•lyuh*
Do you have an adapter for this?	**Tem um adaptador para isto?** *teng oong uh•duhp•tuh•daur puh•ruh ee•stoo*
How do I turn on the lights?	**Como é que se acende as luzes?** *kau•moo eh keh seh uh•sehn•deh uhz loo•zehz*
Could you wake me at...?	**Podia acordar-me às...?** *poo•dee•uh uh•koor•dahr•meh ahz...*
Can I leave this in the safe?	**Posso deixar isto no cofre?** *paw•soo thay•shahr ee•stoo noo kaw•freh*
I'd like to get my things from the safe.	**Queria tirar as minhas coisas do cofre.** *keh•ree•uh tee•rahr uhz mee•nyuhz koy•zuhz thoo kaw•freh*
Is/Are there any mail/ messages for me?	**Há correio/alguma mensagem para mim?** *ah koo•rray•oo/ahl•goo•muh mehn•sah•zseng puh•ruh meeng*
Do you have a laundry service?	**Tem serviço de lavanderia?** *teng sehr•vee•soo deh luh•vuhn•deh•ree•uh*

Problems

There's a problem.	**Há um problema.** *ah oong proo•bleh•muh*
I've lost my key/ key card.	**Perdi a minha chave/carta de chave.** *pehr•dee uh mee•nyuh shahv/kahr•tuh deh shahv*
I've locked myself out of my room.	**Fechei-me fora do quarto.** *fee•shay•meh faw•ruh thoo kwahr•too*
There's no hot water/ toilet paper.	**Não há água quente/papel higiénico.** *nohm ah ah•gwuh kehnt/puh•pehl ee•zseh•nee•koo*
The room is dirty.	**O quarto está sujo.** *oo kwahr•too ee•stah soo•zsoo*
There are bugs in our room.	**Há insetos no quarto.** *ah een•seh•tooz noo kwahr•too*

...doesn't work. **...tem um defeito.** *...teng oong deh•fay•too*
Can you fix...? **Pode arrumar...?** *pawd uh•rroo.mahr...*
the air conditioning **o ar condicionado** *oo ar kawn•dee•seeoo•nah•thoo*
the fan **o ventilador** *oo vehn•tee•luh•daur*
the heat [heating] **o aquecimento** *oo uh•keh•see•mehn•too*
the lights **as luzes** *uhz loo•zehz*
the TV **a TV** *uh teh•veh*
the toilet **o vaso sanitario** *oo vah•zoo suh•nee•tah•rio*
I'd like to move to another room. **Queria mudar de quarto.** *keh•ree•uh moo•dahr deh kwahr•too*

YOU MAY SEE...

EMPURRAR/PUXAR	push/pull
O BANHEIRO/LAVABOS	bathroom/restroom [toilet]
CHUVEIRO	shower
ELEVADOR	elevator [lift]
ESCADAS	stairs
LAVANDERIA	laundry
NÃO PERTURBAR	do not disturb
PORTA DE INCÊNDIO	fire door
SAÍDA (DE EMERGÊNCIA)	(emergency) exit
CHAMADA PARA DESPERTAR	wake-up call

Public restrooms [toilets] can be found in shopping malls, hotels, restaurants, airports, bus stations, the better snack bars and gas stations. You won't find any in the street or in other public places, except for a few along Copacabana beach.

Checking Out

When's check-out? **A que horas temos de deixar o quarto?** *uh kee aw•ruhz teh•mooz deh thay•shahr oo kwahr•too*

Could I leave my bags here until…? **Posso deixar a minha bagagem aqui até…?** *paw•soo day•shahr uh mee•nyuh buh•gah•zseng uh•kee uh•teh…*

Can I have an itemized bill/a receipt? **Pode me dar uma conta detalhada/um recibo?** *pawd meh dahr oo•muh kaum•tuh deh•tuh•lyah•duh/oong reh•see•boo*

I think there's a mistake. **Creio que se enganou.** *kray•oo keh seh ehn•guh•nau*

I'll pay in cash/by credit card. **Pago com dinheiro/com o cartão de crédito.** *pah•goo kaum dee•nyay•roo/kaum oo kuhr•tohm deh kreh•dee•too*

Renting

I reserved an apartment/a room. **Reservei um apartamento/quarto.** *reh•zehr•vay oong uh•puhr•tuh•mehn•too/ kwahr•too*

My name is… **Meu nome é…** *mehoo naum•ee eh…*

Can I have the key/key card? **Posso ter a chave/carta de chave?** *paw•soo tehr uh shahv/kahr•tuh deh shahv*

Are there…? **Tem…?** *teng…*

dishes	**a louça** *uh lau•suh*
pillows	**travesseiros** *truh•veh•say•roo*
sheets	**lençóis** *lehn•soyz*
towels	**toalhas** *too•ah•lyuhz*
utensils [cutlery]	**os talheres** *ooz tuh•lyeh•rehz*
When do I put out the bins/recycling?	**Quando ponho o lixo/o lixo para reciclar lá fora?** *kwuhn•doo paw•nyoo oo lee•shoo/ lee•shoo puh•ruh ree•see•klahr lah faw•ruh*
...is broken.	**...está quebrado** ***m*** **/quebrada** ***f*****.** *...ee•stah keh•brah•doo/ keh•brah•duh*
How does...work?	**Como funciona...?** *kau•moo faun•see•aw•nuh...*
the air conditioner	**o ar condicionado** *oo ar kawn•dee•seeoo•nah•thoo*
the dishwasher	**a máquina de lavar pratos** *uh mah•kee•nuh deh luh•vahr prah•tooz*
the freezer	**o congelador** *oo kaum•zseh•luh•daur*
the heater	**o aquecedor** *oo uh•keh•seh•daur*
the microwave	**o microondas** *oo mee•krau•aun•duhz*
the refrigerator	**a geladeira** *uh zseh•luh•thay•ruh*
the stove	**o fogão** *oo foo•gohm*
the washing machine	**a máquina de lavar (roupa)** *uh mah•kee•nuh deh luh•vahr (rauoo•puh)*

Domestic Items

I need...	**Preciso de...** *preh•see•zoo deh...*
an adapter	**um adaptador** *oong uh•duhp•tuh•daur*
aluminum [kitchen] foil	**papel de alumínio** *puh•pehl deh uh•loo•mee•nee•oo*
a bottle opener	**um abridor de garrafas** *uh•bree•daur deh guh•rrah•fuhz*
a broom	**uma vassoura** *oo•muh vuh•sau•ruh*
a can opener	**um abridor de latas** *ah•bree•daur deh lah•tuhz*

A service charge is generally added to your hotel and restaurant bills. However, if the service has been particularly good, you may want to leave an extra tip. The following is a guide:

Bellman, per bag	R$ 5–10
Hotel maid	R$ 5–10
Restroom attendant	R$ 1–2

The electrical current in Brazil is not completely standardized. Some parts of Brazil are 220 V (Brasília, Florianópolis, Fortaleza, recife, and São Luís), while others, including Rio de Janeiro and São Paulo, are 110 V. Make sure to enquire about the voltage before you plug in any applicances and use an appropriate adaptor if necessary.

cleaning supplies **produtos de limpeza** *prau•thoo•tooz deh leem•peh•zuh*

a corkscrew **um saca-rolhas** *oong sah•kuh•rau•lyuz*

I need... **Preciso de...** *preh•see•zoo deh...*

detergent **detergente em pó para a roupa** *deh•tehr•zsehnt eng paw puh•ruh uh rauoo•puh*

dishwashing liquid **detergente para a louça** *deh•tehr•zsehnt puh•ruh uh lau•suh*

bin bags **sacos para o lixo** *sah•kooz puh•ruh oo lee•shoo*

a light bulb **uma lâmpada elétrica** *oo•muh luhm•puh•duh ee•leh•tree•kuh*

matches **fósforos** *fawz•fuh•rooz*

a mop **o esfregão** *oo ees•fruh•gohm*

paper napkins	**guardanapos de papel** *gwahr•duh•nah•pooz deh puh•pehl*
paper towels	**papel da cozinha** *puh•pehl duh koo•zee•nyuh*
plastic wrap [cling film]	**papel aderente** *puh•pehl uh•deh•rehnt*
a plunger	**um desentupidor** *oong deh•zehn•too•pee•daur*
scissors	**uma tesoura** *oo•muh teh•zau•ruh*
a vacuum cleaner	**um aspirador** *oong uh•spee•ruh•daur*

For In the Kitchen, see page 81.

At the Hostel

Do you have any places left for tonight?	**Ainda há vagas para hoje à noite?** *uh•een•duh ah vah•guhz puh•ruh auzseh ah noyt*
Can I have...?	**Queria...?** *keh•ree•uh...*
a single/double room	**um quarto individual/duplo** *oong kwahr•too een•dee•vee•doo•ahl/doo•ploo*
a blanket	**um cobertor** *oong koo•behr•taur*
a pillow	**um travesseiro** *oong truh•veh•say•roo*
sheets	**lençóis** *lehn•soyz*
a towel	**uma toalha** *oo•muh too•ah•lyuh*
Do you have lockers?	**Tem cacifos?** *teng kuh•see•fooz*
What time are the doors locked?	**A que horas fecham as portas?** *uh keh aw•ruhz feh•shohm uhz pawr•tuhz*

There are over 90 youth hostels (**albergues juveniles**) in Brazil. For a full list of establishments afiliated with Hostelling International, visit www. albergues.com.br.
Hostels are especially popular with backpackers and those traveling on a budget so it is advisable to book well in advance. Many can be found in great beach-side locations.

Do I need a membership card? **Preciso de cartão de sócio?** *preh•see•zoo deh kuhr•tohm deh saw•see•oo*

Here's my international student card. **Aqui está o meu cartão internacional de estudante.** *uh•kee ee•stah oo mehoo kuhr•tohm een•tehr•nuh•seeoo•nahl de ee•stoo•duhnt*

Going Camping

Can I camp here? **Posso acampar aqui?** *paw•soo uh•kuhm•pahr uh•kee*

Where's the campsite? **Onde é o parque de campismo [camping]?** *aund eh oo pahr•keh deh kuhm•peez•moo [kuhm•peeng]*

What is the charge per day/week? **Qual é a tarifa por dia/semana?** *kwahl eh uh tuh•ree•fuh poor dee•uh/seh•muh•nuh*

Are there...? **Há...?** *ah...*

cooking facilities **uma área para se cozinhar** *oo•muh ah•ree•uh puh•ruh seh koo•zee•nyahr*

electrical outlets **electricidade** *ee•leh•tree•see•dahd*

laundry facilities **uma lavanderia** *oo•muh luh•vuhn•deh•ree•uh*

Are there...? **Tem...?** *teng...*

showers **um chuveiro** *oong shoo•vay•roo*

tents for rent [hire] **barracas para alugue** *bah•hah•kaz puh•ruh uh•loo•gehr*

Where can I empty the chemical toilet? **Onde posso esvaziar o banheiro químico?** *aund paw•soo ees•vee•ahr oo buh•nyay•roo kee•mee•koo*

YOU MAY SEE...

ÁGUA POTÁVEL drinking water

É PROIBIDO ACAMPAR no camping

É PROIBIDO ACENDER FOGOS/ CHURRASQUEIRAS no fires/barbecues

Communications

ESSENTIAL

Where's an internet café?	**Onde fica um internet café?** *aund fee•kuh oong een•tehr•neht kuh•feh*
Can I access the Internet here?	**Tenho acesso à internet aqui?** *teh•nyoo uh•seh•soo ah een•tehr•neht uh•kee*
Can I check email here?	**Posso ler o meu e-mail aqui?** *paw•soo lehr oo mehoo ee•mehl uh•khee*
How much per (half) hour?	**Quanto é por (meia) hora?** *kwuhn•too eh poor (may•uh) aw•ruh*
How do I connect/ log on?	**Como conecto/faço o logon?** *kau•moo koo•nehk•too/fah•soo oo law•gawn*
A phone card, please.	**Um cartão telefónico, por favor.** *oong kuhr•tohm tehl•eh•fawn•ee•koo poor fuh•vaur*
Can I have your phone number?	**Pode me dar o seu número de telefone?** *pawd meh dahr oo sehoo noo•meh•roo deh tehl•fawn*
Here's my number/ email address.	**Este é o meu número/e-mail.** *ehst eh oo mehoo noo•meh•roo/ee•mehl*
Call me.	**Telefone-me.** *tehl•fawn•eh•meh*
Email me.	**Envie um e-mail.** *ehn•vee•eh oong ee•mehl*
Hello. This is...	**Alô. Meu nome é...** *aw•lah. Mehoo naum•eh eh...*
I'd like to speak to...	**Queria falar com...** *keh•ree•uh fuh•lahr kaum...*
Could you repeat that, please?	**Poderia repetir, por favor?** *poh•deh•ree•ah reh•peh•teer poor fuh•vaur*
I'll call back later.	**Chamo mais tarde.** *shuh•moo meyez tahr•deh*
Bye.	**Tchau.** *Cha•oo*
Where's the post office?	**Onde são os correios?** *aund sohm ooz koo•rray•ooz*
I'd like to send this to...	**Gostaria de mandar isto para...** *goo•stuh•ree•uh deh muhn•dahr ee•stoo puh•ruh...*

Online

Where's an internet cafe?	**Onde fica um internet café?** *aund fee•kuh oong een•tehr•neht kuh•feh*
Does it have wireless internet?	**Tem internet wireless?** *teng een•tehr•neht wire•less*
What is the WiFi password?	**Qual é a senha do WiFi?** *kwahl eh uh seh•nyuh doo WiFi*
Is the WiFi free?	**O WiFi é grátis?** *oo WiFi eh grah•teez*
Do you have bluetooth?	**Tem bluetooth?** *teng bluetooth*
How do I turn the computer on/off?	**Como ligo/desligo o computador?** *kau•moo lee•goo/dehz•lee•goo oo kaum•poo•tuh•daur*
Can I…?	**Posso…?** *paw•soo…*
access the internet	**acessar a internet** *uh•seh•ssahr uh een•tehr•neht*
check email	**ler o meu e-mail** *lehr oo mehoo ee•mehl*
print	**imprimir** *eeng•pree•meer*
How much per (half) hour?	**Quanto é por (meia) hora?** *kwuhn•too eh poor (may•uh) aw•ruh*
How do I…?	**Como…?** *kau•moo…*
connect/disconnect	**conecto/desconecto** *koo•nehk•too/ dehz•koo•nehk•too*
log on/off	**faço o logon/logoff** *fah•soo oo law•gawn/law•gawf*
type this symbol	**digito este símbolo** *dee•gee•too ehst seem•boo•loo*
What's your email?	**Qual é o seu e-mail?** *kwahl eh oo sehoo ee•mehl*
My email is…	**O meu e-mail é…** *oo mehoo ee•mehl eh…*
Do you have a scanner?	**Tem um scanner?** *teng oong scanner*

Social Media

Are you on Facebook/ Twitter?	**Está no Facebook/Twitter?** *ee•stah noo facebook/twitter*
What's your username?	**Qual é o seu nome de usuário?** *kwahl eh oo sehoo naum•eh deh oo• zuh•ah•ree•uh*
I'll add you as a friend.	**Vou adicioná-lo como amigo.** *vawoo•oo uh•dee•seeoo•nah•loo kau•moo uh•mee•goo*
I'll follow you on Twitter.	**Vou segui-lo no Twitter.** *vawoo•oo seh•gee•loo noo Twitter*
Are you following...?	**Está seguindo...?** *ee•stah uh seh•gheeng•doo...*
I'll put the pictures on Facebook/Twitter.	**Vou colocar as fotos no Facebook/Twitter.** *vawoo koo•loo•khahr uhz faw•tawz noo Facebook/Twitter*
I'll tag you in the pictures.	**Vou te marcar nas fotos.** *vawoo tee•mahr•kahr nuhz faw•tawz*

Phone

A phone card/prepaid phone, please.	**Um cartão de telefone pré-pago, por favor** *oong kuhr•tohm deh tehl•fawn preh•pah•goo poor fuh•vaur*
How much?	**Quanto é?** *kwuhn•too eh*
Where's the pay phone?	**Onde está o telefone pago?** *aund ee•stah oo tehl•fawn pah•goo*
My phone doesn't work here.	**O meu telefone não funciona aqui.** *oo meehoo tehl•fawn nohm foon•seeaw•nuh uh•kee*
What network are you on?	**Em que rede está?** *eng keh rreh•deh ee•stah*
Is it 3G?	**É 3G?** *eh trehz zseh*
I have run out of credit/ minutes.	**Fiquei sem crédito/minutos.** *fee•kay seng kreh•dee•too/mee•noo•tooz*
Can I buy some credit?	**Posso comprar algum crédito?** *paw•soo kaum•prahr ahl•goong kreh•dee•too?*

YOU MAY SEE...

FECHAR	close
APAGAR	delete
E-MAIL	e-mail
SAÍDA	exit
AJUDA	help
MESSENGER	instant messenger
INTERNET	internet
LOGIN	login
(NOVA) MENSAGEM	(new) message
LIGADO/DESLIGADO	on/off
ABRIR	open
IMPRIMIR	print
GUARDAR	save
ENVIAR	send
NOME DO USUÁRIO/SENHA	username/password
INTERNET WIRELESS	wireless internet

Do you have a phone charger? **Tem um carregador de telefone?** *teng oong kah•rreh•guh•daur deh tehl•fawn*

What's the area/ country code for...? **Qual é o código de área/país para...?** *kwahl eh oo kaw•dee•goo deh ah•eh•ree•uh/puh•eez puh•ruh...*

What's the number for Information? **Qual é o número das Informações?** *kwahl eh oo noo•meh•roo duhz eeng•foor•muh•soingz*

I'd like the number for... **Queria o número para...** *keh•ree•uh oo noo•meh•roo puh•ruh...*

I'd like to call collect [reverse the charges]. **Queria telefonar a cobrar no destino.** *keh•ree•uh tehl•fawn•ahr uh koo•brahr noo dehz•tee•noo*

Can I have your number? **Pode me dar o seu número de telefone?** *pawd meh dahr oo sehoo noo•meh•roo deh tehl•fawn*

Here's my number.	**Este é o meu número.** *ehst eh oo mehoo noo•meh•roo*
Call me.	**Me liga.** *meh lee•gah*
Text me.	**Mande uma mensagem de texto.** *muhn•duh oo•muh mehn•sah•zseng deh tehk•stoo*
I'll call you.	**Eu ligo.** *eeoo lee•guh*
I'll text you.	**Mando uma mensagem de texto.** *muhn•doo oo•muh mehn•sah•zseng deh tehk•stoo*

For Numbers, see page 173.

Telephone Etiquette

Hello. This is...	**Alô. Meu nome é...** *ah•lawoo. mehoo nau•mee eh...*
I'd like to speak to...	**Queria falar com...** *keh•ree•uh fuh•lahr kaum...*
Extension...	**Extensão...** *ehs•tehn•sohm...*
Speak louder/more slowly, please.	**Fale mais alto/devagar, por favor.** *fah•leh meyez ahl•too/deh•vuh•gahr poor fuh•vaur*
Could you repeat that?	**Poderia repetir?** *poh.deh.ree.ah reh•peh•teer*
I'll call back later.	**Eu ligo mais tarde.** *eeoo lee•guh meyez tahrd*
Bye.	**Tchau.** *Chah•oo*

For Business Travel, see page 147.

Payphones are easy to use but you will need to purchase a pre-paid calling card. You can buy these from any store displaying a sign reading **Cartão Telefônico Aqui**. Temporary mobile phones with 'pay as you go' plans are also available. The Brazilian internet market is huge and internet cafes can be found throughout the country, although connections in smaller beach resorts can be slow. Many larger hotels provide free WiFi.

YOU MAY HEAR...

Quem fala? *keng fah•luh* Who's calling?

Não desligue. *nohm dehs•lee•geh* Hold on.

Vou ligar agora. *vau lee•gahr uh•gaw•ruh* I'll put you through.

Lamento, mas ele/ela não está. *luh•mehn•too muhz ehl/ehl•uh nohm ee•stah* I'm afraid he's/she's not in.

Ele/Ela não pode atender o telefone. *ehl/ehl•uh nohm pawd uh•tehn•dehr oo tehl•fawn* He/She can't come to the phone.

Quer deixar uma mensagem? *kehr day•shahr oo•muh mehn•sah•zseng* Would you like to leave a message?

Ligue mais tarde/daqui dez minutos. *lee•geh meyez tahr•deh/da•kee•uh dehz mee•noo•tooz* Call back later/in ten minutes.

Ele/Ela pode telefonar para você? *ehl/ehl•uh pawd tehl•fawn•ahr para voh•seh* Can he/she call you back?

Qual é o seu número de telefone? *kwahl eh oo sehoo noo•meh•roo deh tehl•fawn* What's your number?

Fax

Can I send/receive a fax here?	**Posso enviar/receber um fax aqui?** *paw•soo ehn•vee•ahr/reh•seh•behr oong fahks uh•kee*
What's the fax number?	**Qual é o número de fax?** *kwahl eh oo noo•meh•roo deh fahks*
Please fax this to…	**Por favor mande este fax para…** *poor fuh•vaur muhn•deh ehst fahks puh•ruh…*

Post

Where's the post office/mailbox [postbox]?	**Onde é que é o correio/a caixa do correio?** *aund eh keh eh oo koo•rray•oo/uh keye•shuh thoo koo•rray•oo*
A stamp for this postcard/letter, please.	**Um selo para este postal/esta carta, por favor.** *oong seh•loo puh•ruh ehst poo•stahl/eh•stuh kahr•tuh poor fuh•vaur*
How much?	**Quanto é?** *kwuhn•too eh*
I want to send this package by airmail/express.	**Queria mandar este embrulho por via aérea/correio expresso.** *keh•ree•uh muhn•dahr eh•stuh ehm•broo•lyoo poor vee•uh uh•eh•ree•uh/koo•rray•oo ees•preh•soo*
A receipt, please.	**Um recibo, por favor.** *oong reh•see•boo poor fuh•vaur*

Post offices bear the sign ECT (**Empresa de Correios e Telégrafos**) or a sign reading **Correios**; they are generally open from 9:00 a.m. to 5:00 p.m., Mondays through Fridays, and until 1:00p.m. on Saturdays. Street corner mailboxes are yellow.

YOU MAY HEAR...

Por favor preencha a declaração da alfândega. *poor fuh•vaur pree•ehn•shuh uh deh•kluh•ruh•sohm duh uhl•fuhn•dee•guh*	Please fill out the customs declaration form.
Qual é o valor? *kwahl eh oo vuh•laur*	What's the value?
O que é que tem dentro? *oo kee eh keh teng dehn•troo*	What's inside?

Food & Drink

Eating Out

ESSENTIAL

Can you recommend a good restaurant/bar?	**Pode recomendar um bom restaurante/bar?** *pawd reh•kaw•mehn•dahr oong bohng reh•stahoo•ruhnt/bar*
Is there a(n) traditional/ inexpensive restaurant near here?	**Há um restaurante tradicional/ barato perto daqui?** *ah oong reh•stuhoo•ruhnt truh•dee•see•oo•nahl/buh•rah•too pehr•too duh•kee*
A table for…, please.	**Uma mesa para…, por favor.** *oo•muh meh•zuh puh•ruh…poor fuh•vaur*
Could we sit…?	**Podemos sentar…?** *poo•deh•mooz sehn•tahr…*
here/there	**aqui/ali** *uh•kee/uh•lee*
outside	**lá fora** *lah faw•ruh*
in a non-smoking area	**na área para não fumantes** *nuh ah•ree•uh puh•ruh noh-foo•muhnts*
I'm waiting for someone.	**Estou à espera de alguém.** *ee•stawoo ah ee•speh•ruh deh ahl•gehm*
Where's the restroom [toilet]?	**Onde são os banheiros?** *aund sohm ooz buh•nyay•rooz*
A menu, please.	**Uma cardápio, por favor.** *oong car•dah•pee•oo poor fuh•vaur*
What do you recommend?	**O que é que me recomenda?** *oo keh eh keh meh reh•koo•mehn•duh*
I'd like…	**Queria…** *keh•ree•uh…*
Some more…, please.	**Mais…, por favor.** *meyez…poor fuh•vaur*
Enjoy your meal.	**Bom apetite.** *bohng uh•peh•tee•teh*
The check [bill], please.	**A conta, por favor.** *uh kaum•tuh poor fuh•vaur*

Is service included?	**O serviço está incluído?** *oo sehr•vee•soo ee•stah een•kloo•ee•thoo*
Can I pay by credit card?	**Posso pagar com cartão de crédito?** *paw•soo puh•gahr kaum kuhr•tohm deh kreh•dee•too*
Could I have a receipt, please?	**Pode me dar um recibo, por favor?** *pawd meh dahr oong reh•see•boo poor fuh•vaur*
Thank you.	**Obrigado** *m* **/Obrigada** *f***.** *aw•bree•gah•thoo/aw•bree•gah•thuh*

Where to Eat

Can you recommend...?	**Pode recomendar...?** *pawd reh•koo•mehn•dahr...*
a restaurant	**um restaurante** *oong reh•stuhoo•ruhnt*
a bar	**um bar** *oong bar*
a cafe	**um café** *oong kuh•feh*
a fast-food place	**um restaurante de comida rápida [uma rede de fast food]** *oong reh•stuhoo•ruhnt deh koo•mee•duh rah•pee•duh [oo•muh rehd deh fast food]*
a seafood restaurant	**um restaurante de frutos do mar** *oong reh•stuhoo•ruhnt deh froo•tooz doo mahr*
a cheap restaurant	**um restaurante barato** *oong rehz•tahoo•ruhnt buh•rah•too*

an expensive resturant	**um restaurante caro** *oong rehz•tahoo•ruhnt kah•roo*
a restaurant with a good view	**um restaurante com boa vista** *oong rehz•tahoo•ruhnt kaum bau•uh vee•stuh*
an authentic/non-touristy restaurant	**um restaurante típico/não turístico** *oong rehz•tahoo•ruhnt tee•pee•koo/nohm too•ree•stee•koo*

Reservations & Preferences

I'd like to reserve a table...	**Queria reservar uma mesa...** *keh•ree•uh reh•zehr•vahr oo•muh meh•zuh...*
for two	**para dois** *puh•ruh doyz*
for this evening	**para hoje à noite** *puh•ruh auzseh ah noyt*
for tomorrow at...	**para amanhã às...** *puh•ruh uh•muh•nyuh ahz...*
A table for two.	**Uma mesa para dois.** *oo•muh meh•zuh puh•ruh doyz*
We have a reservation.	**Temos uma reserva.** *teh•mooz oo•muh reh•zehr•vuh*
My name is...	**Meu nome é...** *mehoo naum•ee eh...*
Could we sit...?	**Podemos sentar...?** *poo•deh•mooz sehn•tahr...*
here/there	**aqui/ali** *uh•kee/uh•lee*
outside	**lá fora** *lah faw•ruh*
in a non-smoking area	**na área para não-fumantes** *nuh ah•ree•uh puh•ruh noh-foo•muhnts*
by the window	**à janela** *ah zsuh•neh•luh*
in the shade	**à sombra** *ah sohng•bruh*
in the sun	**ao sol** *ahoo sawl*
Where are the restrooms [toilets]?	**Onde são os banheiros?** *aund sohmuhz ooz buh•nyay•rooz*

YOU MAY HEAR...

Tem reserva? *teng reh•sehr•vuh*	Do you have a reservation?
Quantas pessoas? *kwuhn•tuhz peh•sau•uhs*	How many?
Fumante ou não-fumante? *foo•muhnt aw nohmfoo•muhnt*	Smoking or non-smoking?
Deseja encomendar? *deh•zeh•zsuh ehn•caw•mehn•dahr*	Would you like to order?
O que deseja? *oo keh deh•zeh•zsuh*	What would you like?
Recomendo... *reh•koo•mehn•doo...*	I recommend...
Bom apetite. *bohng uh•peh•tee•teh*	Enjoy your meal.

How to Order

Excuse me!	**Por favor!** *poor fuh•vaur*
We're ready to order.	**Estamos prontos para encomendar.** *ee•stuh•mooz prawn•tooz puh•ruh eng•kau•mehn•dahr*
The wine list, please.	**A carta de vinhos, por favor.** *uh kahr•tuh deh vee•nyooz poor fuh•vaur*
I'd like...	**Queria...** *keh•ree•uh...*
a bottle of...	**uma garrafa...** *oo•muh guh•rrah•fuh...*
a carafe of...	**um jarro de...** *oom jah•rroo deh...*
a glass of...	**um copo de...** *oong kaw•poo deh...*
A menu, please.	**Um cardápio, por favor.** *oong car•dah•pee•oo poor fuh•vaur*
Do you have...?	**Tem...?** *teng...*
a menu in English	**um cardápio em Inglês** *oong car•dah•pee•oo eng een•glehz*

a fixed-price menu	**um cardápio, de preço-fixo** *oong car•dah•pee•oo deh preh•soo feek•soo*
a children's menu	**um cardápio de criança** *oong car•dah•pee•oo deh kree•uhn•suh*
What do you recommend?	**O que é que me recomenda?** *oo kee eh keh meh reh•koo•mehn•duh*
What's this?	**O que é isto?** *oo kee eh ee•stoo*
What's in it?	**Leva o quê?** *leh•vuh oo keh*
Is it spicy?	**É picante?** *eh pee•kuhnt*
I'd like…	**Queria…** *keh•ree•uh…*
More…, please.	**Mais…, por favor.** *meyez…poor fuh•vaur*
With/Without…	**Com/Sem…** *kaum/seng…*
I can't have…	**Não posso comer…** *nohm paw•soo koo•mehr…*
rare	**mal passado** *m* **/passada** *f mahl puh•sah•thoo/ puh•sah•thuh*
medium	**meio passado** *m* **/passada** *f may•oo puh•sah•thoo/ puh•sah•thuh*
well-done	**bem passado** *m* **/passada** *f beng puh•sah•thoo/ puh•sah•thuh*
It's to go [take away].	**É para levar.** *eh puh•ruh leh•vahr*

YOU MAY SEE…

COUVERT	cover charge
PREÇO-FIXO	fixed-price
CARDÁPIO	menu
CARDÁPIO DO DIA	menu of the day
SERVIÇO (NÃO) INCLUÍDO	service (not) included
ESPECIAIS	specials

Cooking Methods

baked	**dourado** *m* **/dourada** *f* *dauoo•rah•doo/dauoo•rah•duh*
boiled	**cozido** *m* **/cozida** *f* *koo•zee•thoo/koo•zee•thuh*
braised	**estufado** *m* **/estufada** *f* *ee•stoo•fah•thoo/ee•stoo•fah•thuh*
breaded	**empanado** *m* **/empanada** *f* *ehm•puh•nah•doo/ehm•puh•nah•dah*
creamed	**com natas** *kohng nah•tuhz*
diced	**aos cubos** *ahooz koo•booz*
filet of…	**filete de…** *fee•leht deh…*
fried	**frito** *m* **/frita** *f* *free•too/free•tuh*
grilled	**grelhado** *m* **/grelhada** *f* *gree•lyah•thoo/gree•lyah•thuh*
poached	**escalfado** *m* **/escalfada** *f* *ees•kahl•fah•thoo/ees•kahl•fah•thuh*
roasted	**assado** *m* **/assada** *f* *uh•sah•thoo/uh•sah•thuh*
sautéed	**salteado** *m* **/salteada** *f* *sahl•tee•ah•thoo/sahl•tee•ah•thuh*
smoked	**defumado** *m* **/defumada** *f* *deh•foo•mah•doo/deh•foo•mah•duh*
steamed	**cozido** *m* **/cozida** *f* **a vapor** *koo•zee•thoo/koo•zee•thuh uh vuh•paur*
stewed	**guisado** *m* **/guisada** *f* *gee•zah•thoo/gee•zah•thuh*
stuffed	**recheado** *m* **/recheada** *f* *reh•shee•ah•thoo/reh•shee•ah•thuh*

Dietary Requirements

I am…	**Sou…** *sauoo…*
diabetic	**diabético** *m* **/diabética** *f* *dee•uh•beh•tee•koo/dee•uh•beh•tee•kuh*

lactose intolerant	**intolerante à lactose** *een•tawl•eh•ruhnt ah lahk•tawz*
vegetarian	**vegetariano** *m* **/vegetariana** *f* *veh•zseh•tuh•ree•uh•noo/veh•zseh•tuh•ree•uh•nuh*
vegan	**vegetariano** *veh•geh•tuh•ree•uh•noo*
I'm allergic to…	**Sou alérgico** *m* **/alérgica** *f* **a…** *sauoo uh•lehr•gee•koo/uh•lehr•gee•kuh uh…*
I can't eat…	**Não posso comer…** *nohm paw•soo koo•mehr…*
dairy	**lacticínios** *lahk•tee•see•nee•ooz*
gluten	**glúten** *gloo•tehn*
nuts	**nozes** *naw•zehz*
pork	**carne de porco** *kahrr•neh deh paur•koo*
shellfish	**marisco** *muh•ree•skoo*
spicy foods	**comidas picantes** *koo•mee•duhz pee•kuhnts*
wheat	**trigo** *tree•goo*
Is it halal/kosher?	**É halal/kosher?** *eh uh•lahl/kaw•shehr*
Do you have…?	**Tem…?** *teng…*
skimmed milk	**leite magro** *layt mah•groo*
whole milk	**leite gordo** *layt goahr•doo*
soya milk	**leite de soja** *layt deh saw•zsuh*

The most traditional Brazilian dishes are inspired by Portuguese and African foods, along with the everyday staples: rice, beans and **farihna** (dried, ground cassava). Expect to find seafood, fish, fresh sushi, barbecued meat (**churrasco**), hearty Italian dishes and delicious salads. In many restuarants, portions are large enough to share, and this is acceptable in all but the smartest of places.

Dining with Children

Do you have children's portions?	**Tem porções para crianças?** *teng poor•soings puh•ruh kree•uhn•suhz*
A child's seat, please.	**Um assento de criança, por favor.** *oong uh•sehn•too deh kree•uhn•suh poor fuh•vaur*
Can I have a highchair/ child's seat?	**Tem uma cadeira alta/cadeirinha de criança?** *teng oo•muh kuh•day•ruh ahl•tuh/kuh•day•ree•nyuh deh kree•uhn•suh*
Where can I feed/ change the baby?	**Onde posso alimentar/trocar o bebê [neném]?** *aund paw•soo uh•lee•mehn•tahr/traw•kahr oo beh•beh [neh•neh]*
Can you warm this?	**Pode aquecer isto?** *pawd uh•keh•sehr ee•stoo*

For Traveling with Children, see page 150.

How to Complain

How much longer will our food be?	**Quanto tempo demora a nossa comida?** *kwuhn•too tehm•poo deh•maw•ruh uh naw•suh koo•mee•thuh*
We can't wait any longer.	**Não podemos esperar mais.** *nohm poo•deh•mooz ee•speh•rahr meyez*
We're leaving.	**Vamo embora.** *vuh•moo ehm•baw•ruh*

I didn't order this. **Não encomendei isso.** *nohm ehn•koo•mehn•day ee•soo*

I ordered… **Encomendei…** *ehn•koo•mehn•day…*

I can't eat this. **Não posso comer isto.** *nohm paw•soo koo•mehr ee•stoo*

This is too… **Isto está muito…** *ee•stoo ee•stah mooee•too…*

cold/hot **frio/quente** *free•oo/kehnt*

salty/spicy **salgado/picante** *sahl•gah•thoo/pee•kuhnt*

tough/bland **duro/insosso** *doo•roo/een•saw•soo*

This isn't clean/fresh. **Isto não está limpo/fresco.** *ee•stoo nohm ee•stah leem•poo/frehs•koo*

Paying

The check [bill], please. **A conta, por favor.** *uh kaum•tuh poor fuh•vaur*

Separate checks [bills], please. **Contas separadas, por favor.** *kaum•tuhz seh•puh•rah•duhz poor fuh•vaur*

It's all together. **É tudo junto.** *eh too•doo zsoon•too*

Is service included? **O serviço está incluído?** *oo sehr•vee•soo ee•stah een•kloo•ee•thoo*

What's this amount for? **De que é este valor?** *deh keh eh eh•stuh vuh•loahr*

I didn't have that. I had… **Eu não comi isso. Eu comi…** *ehoo nohm koo•mee ee•soo. ehoo koo•mee…*

Can I pay by credit card? **Posso pagar com cartão de crédito?** *paw•soo puh•gahr kaum kuhr•tohm deh kreh•dee•too*

Can I have an itemized bill/a receipt? **Pode me dar uma conta detalhada/um recibo?** *pawd meh dahr oo•muh kaum•tuh deh•tuh•lyah•duh/oong reh•see•boo*

That was a very good meal. **Foi uma refeição excelente.** *foy oo•muh reh•fay•sohm eh•seh•lehnt*

I've already paid. **Já paguei.** *zsah puh•gay*

Meals & Cooking

O pequeno almoço

Breakfast is usually served from 7:00 to 10:00 a.m. It can include coffee, rolls, butter and jam, along with fresh fruit juice, fruit, toast and pastries.

O almoço

Lunch is the main meal of the day, served from12:30 to 2:30 p.m. Shops are normally closed during these hours. In Brazilian resorts, lunch is often served without interruption from12:30 until the evening. It generally includes soup or salad, fish or meat, and a dessert.

O jantar

Dinner is served from about 8:00 to 11:00 p.m. It typically includes soup, fish or meat, salad, bread, and fruit or a sweet for dessert. Coffee or espresso is almost always served at the end of the meal.

Breakfast

a água *uh ah•gwuh*	water
o bolinho *oo bau•lee•nyoo*	muffin
o café.../chá... *oo kuh•feh.../shah...*	coffee.../tea...
com açúcar *kaum uh•soo•kuhr*	with sugar
com adoçante artificial *kaum uh•thoo•suhnt uhr•tee•fee•see•ahl*	with artificial sweetner
com leite *kaum layt*	with milk
descafeínado *dehz•kuh•fay•nah•thoo*	decaf
cafezinho *kuh•feh•zee•nyoo*	black
as carnes frias *uhz kahr•nehz free•uhz*	cold cuts [charcuterie]
o cereal (frio/quente) *oo seh•ree•ahl (free•oo/kehnt)*	(cold/hot) cereal

a geleia *ah zseh•lay•uh*	jam
a farinha de aveia *uh fuh•ree•nyuh deh uh•vay•uh*	oatmeal
o leite *oo layt*	milk
a manteiga *uh muhn•tay•guh*	butter
a omelete *uh aw•meh•leh•tuh*	omelet
o iogurte *uh yaw•goort*	yogurt
o ovo… *oo au•voo…*	…egg
muito fervido/fervido macio *mooee•too fehr•vee•thoo/fehr•vee•thoo muh•see•oo*	hard-boiled/ soft-boiled
estrelado [frito] *ee•struh•lah•doo [free•too]*	fried
mexido *meh•shee•doo*	scrambled
o pão *oo pohm*	bread
o pãozinho *oo pohm•zee•nyoo*	roll
o queijo *oo kay•zsoo*	cheese
as salsichas *uhz sahl•see•shuhz*	sausages
o suco de… *oo soo•koo deh*	…juice
fruta *froo•tuh*	fruit
maçã *muh•suh*	apple
toranja *uh taw•ruhn•zsuh*	grapefruit
laranja *luh•ruhn•zsuh*	orange
o toucinho *oo taw•see•nyoo*	bacon
as torradas *uhz too•rrah•duhz*	toast
o jogurte *oo yaw•goort*	yogurt

Appetizers

as carnes frias *uhz kahr•nehz free•uhz*	cold cuts
o chouriço *oo shauoo•ree•soo*	sausage
as lulas à milanesa *uhz loo•luhz ah mee•luh•neh•zuh*	squid
o paio *oo peye•oo*	smoked pork fillet

os pimentões assados *ooz pee•mehn•toehnz uh•sah•dooz* roasted peppers
o pipis *oo pee•peez* spicy chicken stew
siri recheada *see•ree eh•shee•ah•thuh* stuffed crab

Soup

o caldo verde *oo kahl•doo vehrd* potato and kale soup with sausage
o gaspacho *oo guhz•pah•shoo* chilled soup with tomatoes, sweet peppers, onions, cucumbers and croutons
a sopa de bacalhau *a sau•puh buh•kuh•lyahoo* dried cod soup with garlic and bread
a sopa de pão *a sau•puh duh pohm* bread soup with garlic and herbs
a sopa de carne com legumes e macarrão *a sau•puh deh kahrn kaum leh•goomz eh muh•kuh•rrohm* meat broth with vegetables and macaroni
a sopa seca *uh sau•puh seh•kuh* thick soup with meat, cabbage and bread
a sopa transmontana *a sau•puh truhnz•moo•tuh•nuh* vegetable soup with bacon and bread
a sopa... *uh sau•puh...* ...soup
- **à pescador** *ah pehs•kuh•daur* fish
- **canja** *keng•zsuh* chicken and rice
- **de abóbora** *deh uh•baw•buh•ruh* pumpkin
- **de agriões** *deh uh•gree•oings* potato and watercress
- **de coentro** *deh koo•eng•troo* coriander, bread, and poached eggs
- **de ervilha** *deh eer•vee•lyuh* green pea

Fish & Seafood

o atum *oo uh•toong*	tuna
as amêijoas à Bulhão Pato *uhz uh•may•zsoo•uhz ah boo•lyohm pah•too*	clams with coriander, garlic and onion
as amêijoas à Portuguesa *uhz uh•may•zsoo•uhz ah poor•too•geh•zuh*	clams with garlic, parsley and olive oil
o bacalhau à Gomes de Sá *oo buh•kuh•lyahoo ah gau•mehz deh sah*	dried cod with olives, garlic, onions, parsley and hard-boiled eggs
o bacalhau podre *oo buh•kuh•lyahoo pau•dreh*	baked layers of cod and fried potatoes
a cabeça de pescada cozida *uh kuh•beh•suh deh peh•skah•thuh koo•zee•thuh*	fish stew
os camarões… *ooz kuh•muh•roings…*	…shrimp [prawns]
fritos *free•tooz*	fried
grandes *gruhn•dehz*	large [king]
no espeto *noo ee•speh•too*	on a stick
a caldeirada… *uh kahl•day•rah•thuh…*	fish with onions, tomatoes, potatoes, olive oil…
à fragateira *ah fruh•guh•tay•ruh*	shellfish and mussels in a fish stock with tomatoes

A popular Portuguese import is **bacalhau** (dried, salted cod). On sale in shops and markets, it looks like sheets of stiff, gray cardboard, but when soaked and cooked it is transformed. It is regularly seen on menus as **bolinhos de bacalhau**, meltingly rich rissoles (croquettes). Also look out for **cozido**, another Portuguese dish made up of stewed meats and vegetables served with broth.

à moda da Póvoa *ah maw•duh duh praw•voo•uh*	hake, skate, sea bass and eel
o espadarte *oo ees•puh•dahrt*	swordfish
a lagosta *uh luh•gau•stuh*	lobster
a lampreia *uh luhm•pray•uh*	lamprey
o linguado *oo leeng•gwah•thoo*	sole
as lulas *uhz loo•luhz*	squid
as lulas recheadas *uhz loo•luhz reh•shee•ah•duhz*	stuffed squid
os mariscos *ooz muh•rees•kooz*	seafood
a moqueca de peixe *uh moo•keh•kuh deh paysh*	stew made of fish, shellfish or shrimp with coconut milk
as ostras *uhz aw•struhz*	oysters in butter and wine
o pargo *oo pahr•goo*	bream
o polvo *oo paul•voo*	octopus
o vatapá *oo vuh•tuh•pah*	fish and shrimp in a paste made of flour or breadcrumbs

Meat & Poultry

o arroz de frango *oo uh•rrauz deh fruhn•goo*	chicken with white wine, ham and rice
o bife [filé] *oo beef [fee•leh]*	steak
o bife na frigideira *oo beef nuh free•zsuh•day•ruh*	steak fried in butter, white wine and garlic
o carneiro *oo kuhr•nay•roo*	lamb
a carne de porco *uh kahrn deh paur•koo*	pork
a carne de sol com feijão verde *uh kahrn deh sol kaum fay•zsohm vehrd*	sun-dried meat (jerky) with green beans
a carne de vaca *uh kahrn deh vah•kuh*	beef
o carneiro guisado [ensopado] *oo kuhrr•nay•roo gee•zah•thoo [eng•soo•pah•do]*	mutton with tomatoes, garlic and herbs
o coelho *oo koo•eh•lyoo*	rabbit
a costeleta *uh koo•stuh•leh•tuh*	cutlet
o cozido à Portuguesa *oo koo•zee•doo ah poor•too•geh•zuh*	boiled beef, bacon, smoked sausage and vegetables
a feijoada *uh fay•zsoo•ah•duh*	Brazil's national dish: black beans cooked with bacon, salted pork, jerky and sausage
o frango *oo fruhn•goo*	chicken
o frango na púcara *oo fruhn•goo nuh poo•keh•ruh*	chicken stewed in port and cognac, then fried with almonds
o medalhão *uh meh•duh•lyohm*	tenderloin steak
a perdiz à caçador *oo pehr•deez uh kuh•suh•daur*	partridge simmered with carrots, onions, white wine and herbs
o presunto *oo preh•zoon•too*	cured ham

as tripas à moda do Porto *uhz tree•puhz ah maw•duh thoo paur•too* tripe cooked with pork, beans and chicken
a vitela *uh vee•tehl•uh* veal
o xinxim de galinha *oo sheeng•sheeng deh guh•lee•nyuh* chicken cooked in dried shrimp, peanuts and parsley

Vegetables & Staples

o açafrão *oo uh•suh•frohm* saffron
o acarajé *oo uh•kuh•ruh•zseh* grated beans fried in palm oil, served with pepper sauce, onions and shrimp
o açúcar *oo uh•soo•kuhr* sugar
as alcaparras *uhz ahl•kuh•pah•rruhz* capers
a alface *uh ahl•fah•seh* lettuce
as amêndoas *uhz uh•mehn•doo•uhz* almonds
o arroz... *oo uh•rrauz...* rice...
  de alhos *deh ah•lyooz* with garlic
  de cozido *deh koo•zee•thoo* cooked in meat stock
  de feijão *de fay•zsohm* with beans
as batatas... *uhz buh•tah•tuhz...* potatoes...
  cozidas *koo•zee•duhz* boiled
  cozidas com pele *koo•zee•duhz kohm pehl* boiled in their skins
  fritas *free•tuhz* fries [chips]
  de palha *deh pah•lyuh* matchsticks
o puré de batatas *oo poo•reh deh buh•tah•tuhz* mashed potatoes
as cebolas *uhz seh•bau•luhz* onions
os cogumelos *ooz koo•goo•meh•looz* mushrooms
as ervilhas *uhz eer•vee•lyuhz* peas
a farinha *uh fuh•ree•nyuh* flour
as favas *uhz fah•vuhz* broad beans
o feijão *oo fay•zsohm* kidney beans

o feijão verde *oo fay•zsohm vehrd* green beans
o manjericão *oo muhn•zseh•ree•kohm* basil
a manteiga *uh muhn•tay•guh* butter
as massas *uhz mah•suhz* pasta
o pão *oo pohm* bread
os pimentões *ooz pee•mehn•toehnz* peppers
o rutu à mineira *oo rroo•too ah mee•nay•ruh* beans, cassava, flour, pork, cabbage, fried eggs and bacon
a salsa *uh sahl•suh* parsley

Fruit

o abacate *oo uh•buh•kaht* avocado
o abacaxi *oo uh•buh•kah•shee* pineapple
damascos *oo duh•mahs•koo* apricots
as ameixas *uhz uh•may•shuhz* plums
o oxicoco *oo okzee•kaw•koouh* cranberry
a banana *uh buh•nuh•nuh* banana
as cerejas *uhz seh•ray•zsuhz* cherries
o coco *oo kaw•koo* coconut
a framboesa *uh fruhm•booeh•zuh* raspberry

a fruta *uh froo•tuh* fruit
a goiaba *uh goy•ah•buh* guava
o kiwi *oo kee•wee* kiwi
a laranja *uh luh•ruhn•zsuh* orange
a lima *uh lee•muh* lime
o limão *oo lee•mohm* lemon
a maçã *uh muh•suh* apple
o mamão *oo muh•mohm* papaya
a manga *uh muhn•guh* mango
a mexerica *uh meh•sheh•ree•kuh* tangerine
a melancia *uh muh•luhn•see•uh* watermelon
o melão *oo meh•lohm* melon
o mirtilo *oo meer•tee•loo* blueberry
os morangos *ooz moo•ruhn•gooz* strawberries
a pêra *uh peh•ruh* pear
o pêssego *oo pay•seh•goo* peach
a toranja *uh taw•ruhn•zsa* grapefruit
as uvas *uhz oo•vuhz* grapes

Cheese

o azeitão *oo uh•zay•tohm* creamy cheese
a bola *uh bau•luh* hard cow's milk cheese
o cabreiro *oo kuh•bray•roo* goat's milk cheese
o castelo branco *oo kuh•steh•loo bruhn•koo* creamy blue cheese
a évora *uh eh•voo•ruh* creamy cheese
a ilha *uh ee•lyuh* cow's milk cheese from the Azores Islands (Portugal)
o queijo *oo kay•zsoo* cheese
o queijo de Minas *oo•kay•zsoo deh mee•nuhz* Brazilian cow's milk cheese
o requeijão *oo reh•kay•zsohm* creamy Brazilian cheese
o serra *oo she•rruh* creamy goat's milk cheese

macio *muh•see•oo* soft
duro *doo•roo* hard
suave *swahv* mild
forte *fawrt* strong

Dessert

a arrufada de Coimbra *uh uh•rroo•fah•duh deh kooeem•bruh* cinnamon dough cake
a babá-de-moça *uh buh•bah deh mau•suh* dessert made of egg yolk, coconut milk and syrup
o bolo podre *oo bau•loo pau•dreh* honey and cinnamon cake
as broas castelares *uhz brau•uhz kuh•steh•lah•rehz* sweet-potato biscuits
a canjica *uh kuhn•zsee•kuh* dessert made with sweet corn and milk
a goiabada *uh goy•uh•bah•duh* thick paste made of guavas
a mousse de maracujá *uh moo•seh deh muh•ruh•koo•zsah* passion fruit mousse
os ovos moles *ooz aw•vooz mawlz* egg yolks cooked in syrup
o pastel de Tentúgal *oo puhz•tehl deh tehn•too•gahl* pastry filled with egg yolks cooked in syrup
pudim *poo•deeng* caramel custard
quindim *keeng•deeng* coconut and egg yolk pudding

Sauces & Condiments

o sal *o sahl* salt
a pimenta *uh pee•mehn•tuh* pepper
mostarda *mooz•tahr•duh* mustard
ketchup *ket•chup* ketchup

At the Market

Where are the trolleys/ baskets?	**Onde estão os carrinhos/cestos?** *aund ee•stohm ooz kuh•rree•nyooz/sehs•tooz*
Where is...?	**Onde é...?** *aund eh...*
I'd like some of that/ those.	**Queria isso/esses.** *keh•ree•uh ee•soo/eh•sehz*
Can I taste it?	**Posso provar?** *paw•soo proo•vahr*
I'd like...	**Queria...** *keh•ree•uh...*
a kilo/half-kilo of...	**um quilo/meio quilo de...** *oong kee•loo/may•oo kee•loo deh...*
a liter/half-liter of...	**um litro/meio litro de...** *oong lee•troo/may•oo lee•troo deh...*
I'd like...	**Queria...** *keh•ree•uh...*
a piece of...	**uma fatia de...** *oo•muh fuh•tee•uh deh...*
a slice of...	**um pedaço de...** *oong peh•dah•soo deh...*
More./Less.	**Mais./Menos.** *meyez/meh•nooz*
How much?	**Quanto é?** *kwuhn•too eh*
Where do I pay?	**Onde pago?** *aund pah•goo*
A bag, please.	**Um saco, por favor.** *oong sah•koo poor fuh•vaur*
I'm being helped.	**Alguém estáme ajudando.** *ahl•geng ee•stah meh uh•zsoo•dahn•doo*

YOU MAY HEAR...

Deseja alguma coisa? *deh•zeh•zsuh ahl•goo•muh coy•zuh*	Would you like something?
O que é que deseja? *oo kee eh keh deh•zeh•zsuh*	What would you like?
Mais alguma coisa? *meyez ahl•goo•muh coy•zuh*	Anything else?
São...reais. *sohm...ree•eyez*	That's...reais.

In the Kitchen

bottle opener	**o abridor de garrafas** *oo uh•bree•daur deh guh•rrah•fuhz*
bowl	**a tijela** *tee•jeh•lah*
can opener	**o abridor de latas** *oo ah•bree•daur deh lah•tuhz*
corkscrew	**o saca-rolhas** *oo sah•kuh rau•lyuhz*
cups	**as xícaras** *uhz shee•kuh•ruhz*
forks	**os garfos** *ooz gahr•fooz*

Brazil and coffee go hand-in-hand and coffee is one of the country's most successsful exports. Brazilian coffee is roasted dark, ground fine, prepared strong, and drunk with plenty of sugar. **Café com leite** (coffee with hot milk) is the traditional breakfast drink. After breakfast, it is served black in tiny **demitasses** (cups). These **cafezinhos** or little coffees are served piping hot at all **botequins**. Decaffeinated coffee can be found in supermarkets but is difficult to come across in restaurants.

YOU MAY SEE...

USAR ATÉ...	best if used by...
CALORIAS	calories
SEM GORDURA	fat free
MANTER REFRIGERADO	keep refrigerated
PODE CONTER VESTÍGIOS DE...	may contain traces of...
MICROONDAS	microwaveable
DATA DE VENDA...	sell by...
PRÓPRIO PARA VEGETARIANOS	suitable for vegetarians

frying pan	**a frigideira** *uh free•zsee•thay•ruh*
glasses	**os copos** *ooz kaw•pooz*
knife	**as facas** *uhz fah•kuhz*
measuring cup/spoon	**o copo/a colher de medir** *oo kaw•poo/uh koo•lyehr deh meh•deer*
paper napkin	**o guardanapo de papel** *oo gwahr•duh•nah•poo deh puh•pehl*
plates	**os pratos** *ooz prah•tooz*
pot	**a panela** *uh puh•neh•luh*
saucepan	**a caçarola** *uh kuh•suh•rawl•uh*
spatula	**a espátula** *uh ees•pah•too•luh*
spoon	**as colheres** *uhz koo•lyeh•rehz*

Drinks

ESSENTIAL

The wine list/drink menu, please.	**A carta de vinhos/cardápio de bebidas, por favor.** *uh kahr•tuh deh vee•nyooz/car•dah•pee•oo deh beh•bee•duhz poor fuh•vaur*
What do you recommend?	**O que me recomenda?** *oo keh meh reh•koo•mehn•duh*
I'd like a bottle/glass of red/white wine.	**Queria uma garrafa/um copo de vinho tinto/branco.** *keh•ree•uh oo•muh guh•rrah•fuh/oong kaw•poo deh vee•nyoo teen•too/bruhn•koo*
The house wine, please.	**O vinho da casa, por favor.** *oo vee•nyoo duh kah•zuh poor fuh•vaur*
Another bottle/glass, please.	**Outra garrafa/Outro copo, por favor.** *auoo•truh guh•rrah•fuh/auoo•troo kaw•poo poor fuh•vaur*
I'd like a local beer.	**Gostaria de uma cerveja local.** *goo•stuh•ree•uh deh oo•muh sehr•vay•zsuh loo•kahl*
Can I buy you a drink?	**Posso oferecer uma bebida?** *paw•soo aw•freh•sehr oo•muh beh•bee•thuh*
Cheers!	**Saúde!** *Sah•ood*
A coffee/tea, please.	**Um café/chá, por favor.** *oong kuh•feh/shah poor fuh•vaur*
Black.	**Cafezinho.** *kuh•feh•zee•nyoo*
With...	**com...** *kaum...*
milk	**leite** *layt*
sugar	**açúcar** *uh•soo•kuhr*
artificial sweetener	**adoçante** *uh•doo•suhnty*
A..., please.	**..., por favor.** *...por fuh•vaur*
juice	**Um suco** *oong soo•koo*
soda	**Um refrigerante** *oong reh•freh•zhay•rahnt*

sparkling/still water	**Uma água com/sem gás** *oo-muh ah•gwuh kaum/sehm gahz*
Is the tap water safe to drink?	**A água da torneira é boa para beber?** *uh ah•gwuh duh toor•nay•ruh eh baw•uh puh•ruh beh•behr*

Non-alcoholic Drinks

a água de coco *uh ah•gwuh deh kau•koo*	coconut juice
a água com/sem gás *uh ah•gwuh kaum/ sehn gahz*	carbonated/ noncarbonated [still] water
o chá frio *oo shah free•oo*	iced tea
o café *oo kuh•feh*	coffee
o caldo de cana *oo kahl•doo deh kuh•nuh*	sugar-cane juice
o leite *oo layt*	milk
o leite de coco *oo layt deh kau•koo*	coconut milk
o suco *oo soo•koo*	juice
o refrigerante *oo reh•free•zhay•rahnt*	soda

YOU MAY HEAR...

Posso oferecer-lhe uma bebida? *paw•soo aw•freh•sehr•lyeh oo•muh beh•bee•thuh*	Can I get you a drink?
Com leite/açúcar? *kaum layt/uh•soo•kuhr*	With milk/sugar?
Água com ou sem gás? *ah•gwuh kaum auoo seng gahz*	Carbonated or non-carbonated [still] water?

Look for the bars advertising **suco** (juice) with lots of fresh fruit on display. **Sumol®** is the oldest brand name of fruit juice and is found in almost every shop selling food. It is a lightly carbonated orange drink.

Aperitifs, Cocktails & Liqueurs

aguardente de... *ah•gwahr•thent deh...*	tequila with...
figo *fee•goo*	fig
medronho *meh•draw•nyoo*	arbutus berry (a small strawberry-like fruit)
velha *veh•lyuh*	brandy
a batida... *uh buh•tee•duh...*	cane spirit with fruit juice, sugar, ice and...
de cajú *deh kuh•zsoo*	cashew nut
de coco *deh kau•koo*	coconut
de maracujá *deh muh•ruh•koo•zsah*	passion fruit
a caipirinha *uh keye•pee•ree•nyuh*	cane spirit, crushed lime, sugar and ice
a Cuba livre *uh koo•buh lee•vreh*	rum and Coke®
a gin *uh gzseeng*	gin
a ginjinha *uh zseeng•zsee•nyuh*	spirit distilled from morello cherries
o uísque *oo wees•keh*	whiskey
o vermute *oo vehr•moot*	vermouth
a tequila *uh teh•kee•luh*	tequila
o rum *oo roong*	rum
a vodca *uh vaw•dee•kuh*	vodka

Beer

a cerveja *uh sehr•vay•zsuh*	beer
a cerveja branca *uh sehr•vay•zsuh bruhn•kuh*	lager
a cerveja preta *uh sehr•vay•zsuh preh•tuh*	dark beer
cerveja leve *sehr•veh•zsuh leh•veh*	light beer
um chope *oo shaw•pee*	draft [draught] beer
engarrafada *ehn•guh•rruh•fah•duh*	bottled
local/importada *loo•kahl/eem•pawr•tah•duh*	local imported
sem álcool *seng ahl•kawl*	non-alcoholic

Beer is a popular drink in Brazil. Try local brew **Antártica**. It is often served with **tremoços** (salted lupini beans) or **amendoins** (peanuts). **Cachaça** is the national spirit and comes in varying degrees of quality. It is made from the juice of cane sugar. The very best compare favorably to a top whiskey or brandy. The famous **caipirinha** cocktail is based on this.

Wine

o vinho... *oo vee•nyoo...*	...wine
de casa/mesa *deh kah•zuh/meh•zuh*	house/table
(da) Madeira *(thuh) muh•thay•ruh*	(from) Madeira
(do) Porto *(thoo) paur•too*	Port
espumante *ee•spoo•muhnt*	sparkling
seco/doce *seh•koo/dau•seh*	dry/sweet
tinto/branco/rosé *teen•too/bruhn•koo/raw•zeh*	red/white/blush [rosé]
verde *vehrd*	dry white wine

Brazil turns out some good red and white wines from its vineyards in the South. Labels to look for include **Almadén** and **Forestier**.

On the Menu

o abacate *oo uh•buh•kaht* avocado
o abacaxi *oo uh•buh•kah•shee* pineapple
a abóbora *uh uh•baw•boo•ruh* pumpkin
o açafrão *oo uh•suh•frohm* saffron
o acarajé *oo uh•kuh•ruh•zseh* fried beans
o açúcar *oo uh•soo•kuhr* sugar
o agrião *oo uh•gree•ohm* watercress
a água *uh ah•gwuh* water
a água com gás *uh ah•gwuh kohn gahz* carbonated mineral water
a água de coco *uh ah•gwuh deh kau•koo* coconut juice
a água mineral *uh ah•gwuh mee•neh•ral* mineral water
o aipo *oo ah•ee•poo* celery
a alcachofra *uh ahl•kuh•shau•fruh* artichoke
as alcaparras *uhz ahl•kuh•pah•rruhz* capers
o alecrim *oo uh•leh•kreeng* rosemary
a aletria *uh uhl•eh•tree•uh* sweet noodle pudding
a alface *uh ahl•fah•seh* lettuce
a alheira *uh ah•lwyay•ruh* sausage
o alho *oo ah•lyoo* garlic
o alho poró *oo ah•lyoo pau•rroh* leek
o almoço *oo ahl•mau•soo* lunch
as almôndegas *uhz ahl•mawn•deh•guhz* fishballs or meatballs
as amêijoas *uhz uh•may•zsoo•uhz* baby clams
as ameixas *uhz uh•may•shuhz* plums
as ameixas secas *uhz uh•may•shuhz seh•kuhz* prunes
a amêndoa *uh uh•mehn•doo•uh* almond
o amendoim *oo uh•mehn•doo•eeng* peanut
a amora *uh uh•maw•ruh* blackberry
a anchova *uh uhn•shau•vuh* anchovy

o aperitivo *oo uh•pehr•uh•tee•voo* aperitif
o arenque *oo uh•rehn•keh* herring
o arroz *oo uh•rrauz* rice
o arroz doce *oo uh•rrauz dau•seh* rice pudding
os aspargos *ooz ees•pahr•gooz* asparagus
o assado *oo uh•sah•thoo* roast
o atum *oo uh•toong* tuna
a aveia *uh uh•vay•uh* oats
a avelã *uh uh•veh•luh* hazelnut
as aves *uhz ahv•ehz* poultry
a azeda *uh uh•zeh•duh* sorrel
azedo *uh•zeh•thoo* sour
o azeite *oo uh•zay•teh* oil
az azeitonas *uhz uh•zay•tau•nuhz* olive
o bacalhau *oo buh•kuh•lyahoo* cod
a banana *uh buh•nuh•nuh* banana
a batata *uh buh•tah•tuh* potato
a batata doce *uh buh•tah•tuh dau•seh* sweet potato
as batatas fritas *uhz buh•tah•tuhz free•tuhz* fries [chips]
a baunilha *uh bahoo•nee•lyuh* vanilla
a bebida *uh beh•bee•thuh* drink

o berbigão *oo behr•bee•gohm* type of cockle
a beringela *uh behr•eeng•zseh•luh* eggplant [aubergine]
o besugo *oo beh•soo•goo* bream(fish)
a beterraba *uh beh•teh•rrah•buh* beet [beetroot]
o bife *oo beef* steak
o bife acebolado *oo beef uh•seh•boo•lah•thoo* steak with onions
a bola de Berlim *uh bau•luh deh behr•leeng* doughnut
a bolacha *uh boo•lah•shuh* cookie [biscuit]
a bolacha de água e sal *uh boo•lah•shuh deh ah•gwuh ee sahl* cracker
o bolo *oo bau•loo* pastry
o borrego *oo boo•rreh•goo* lamb
as broas de batata doce *uhz brau•uhz duh buh•tah•tuh dau•seh* sweet-potato cookies
as broas de mel *uhz brau•uhz deh mehl* corn flour and honey cookies
os brócolis *ooz bruw•koo•looz* broccoli
os bunuelos *ooz boo•noo•eh•leez* dough fritters
o cabrito *oo kuh•bree•too* kid
a caça *uh kah•suh* game
o cacau *oo kuh•kahoo* cocoa
o cachorro quente *oo kuh•shau•roo kehnt* hot dog
o café *oo kuh•feh* coffee
o caju *oo kah•zsoo* cashew nut
a caldeirada *uh kahl•day•rah•duh* fish stew
o caldo *oo kahl•doo* consommé
o caldo de cana *oo kahl•doo deh kuh•nuh* sugar-cane juice
o caldo verde *oo kahl•doo vehrd* potato and kale soup
os camarões *ooz kuh•muh•roings* shrimp
o canapé *oo kuh•nuh•peh* small open sandwich
a canela *uh kuh•neh•luh* cinnamon
a canja *uh keng•juh* chicken soup with rice

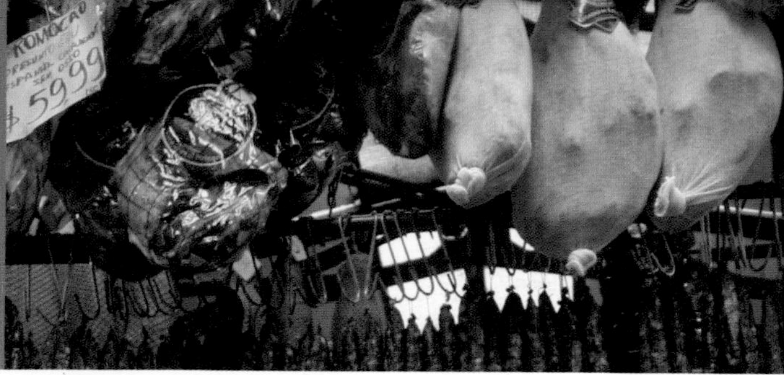

o capão *oo cuh•pohm* capon
o caqui *oo kuh•kee* persimmon
o caracol *oo kuh•ruh•kawl* snail; spiral bun with currants
o caranguejo *oo kuh•ruhn•gay•zsoo* crab
o carapau *oo kuh•ruh•pahoo* mackerel
o caril *oo kuh•reel* curry powder
a carne de porco *uh kahr•neh deh paur•koo* pork
a carne de sol *uh kahr•neh deh sawl* sun-dried meat, jerky
a carne de vaca *uh kahr•neh deh vah•kuh* beef
a carne picada *uh kahr•neh pee•kah•thuh* minced meat
o carneiro *oo kuhrr•nay•roo* mutton
as carnes *uhz kahr•nehz* meat
as carnes frias *uhz kahr•nehz free•uhz* [charcuterie] cold cuts
o caruru *oo kuh•roo•roo* minced herbs in oil and spices
caseiro *oo kuh•zay•roo* homemade
a casquinha de siri *uh kuhz•kee•nyuh deh see•ree* crab in its shell
a castanha *uh kuhz•tuh•nyuh* chestnut
a castanha de caju *uh kuhz•tuh•nyuh deh kah•zsoo* cashew nut

a cavala *uh kuh•vuh•luh*	mackerel
a cebola *uh seh•bau•luh*	onion
a cenoura *uh seh•nau•ruh*	carrot
a cereja *uh seh•ray•zsuh*	cherry
o chá *oo shah*	tea
o chá com leite *oo shah kaum layt*	tea with milk
o chá com limão *oo shah kaum lee•mohm*	tea with lemon
o chá de limão *oo shah deh lee•mohm*	tea made from lemon peel infusion
o chá maté *oo shah muh•teh*	tea infused with maté-tree leaf
o cherne *oo shehr•neh*	black grouper
a chicória *uh shee•kaw•ree•uh*	chicory
o chispe *oo sheez•peh*	pig's foot [trotter]
o chocolate quente *oo shoo•koo•laht kehnt*	hot chocolate
os chocos *ooz shau•kooz*	cuttlefish
o chouriço *oo shaw•ree•soo*	smoked pork sausage
o chuchu *oo shoo•shoo*	type of rutabaga
o churrasco *oo shoo•rahz•koo*	charcoal-grilled meat
as cocadas *uhz caw•cah•duhz*	coconut macaroons
o coco *oo kau•koo*	coconut
a codorna *uh koo•dawrr•nuh*	quail
o coelho *oo koo•eh•lyoo*	rabbit
o coentro *oo koo•ehn•troo*	coriander
o cogumelo *oo koo•goo•meh•loo*	button mushroom
o colorau *oo koo•loo•rahoo*	paprika
os cominho *ooz koo•mee•nyoo*	cumin
a compota *uh koom•paw•tuh*	compote, stewed fruit
os condimentos *ooz kaum•dee•mehn•tooz*	seasonings
o congro *oo kaum•groo*	conger eel
o conhaque *oo kaw•nyahk*	cognac

a conta *uh kaum•tuh*	bill
o copo *oo kaw•poo*	glass
o coração *oo koo•ruh•sohm*	heart
o cordeiro *oo koor•day•roo*	lamb
a corvina *uh kawr•vee•nuh*	croaker (fish)
a costeleta *uh koo•stuh•leh•tuh*	cutlet
a couve *uh kaw•veh*	cabbage
a couve Portuguesa *uh kaw•veh poor•too•geh•zuh*	kale
a couve roxa *uh kaw•veh rau•shuh*	red cabbage
a couve-de-bruxelas *uh kaw•veh de broo•sheh•luhz*	brussels sprouts
a couve-flor *uh kaw•veh flaur*	cauliflower
a coxinha de galinha *uh kaw•shee•nyuh deh guh•lee•nyuh*	pastry filled with chicken
os cravinhos *ooz kruh•vee•nyooz*	cloves
o creme *oo krehm*	cream
o creme de abacate *oo krehm deh uh•buh•kaht*	avocado with lime juice and sugar
o creme inglês *oo krehm eeng•laez*	custard
o crepe *oo krehp*	pancake
a criação *uh kree•uh•sohm*	poultry
cru *kroo*	raw
os crustáceos *ooz kroo•stah•see•ooz*	shellfish
o damasco *oo duh•mahs•koo*	apricot
a dendê *uh dehn•deh*	palm oil
o doce de abóbora *oo thaus deh uh•baw•boo•ruh*	pumpkin dessert
a geleia *uh zseh•lay•uh*	jam
o doce de laranja *oo thaus de luh•ruhn•zsuh*	marmalade

o doce de ovos e amêndoa *oo thaus deh aw•vooz ee uh•mehn•doo•uh*	marzipan
a empadinha *uh eem•puh•thee•nyuh*	filled pastry
o empadão de batata *oo eem•puh•dohm deh buh•tah•tuh*	shepherd's pie
empanado *ehm•puh•nah•doo*	breaded
a enguia *uh eng•gee•uh*	eel
o ensopado de cabrito *oo eng•soo•pah•thoo deh keh•bree•too*	kid stew
a entrada *uh ehn•trah•thuh*	appetizer [starter]
o entrecosto *oo ehn•treh•kaus•too*	sparerib
a erva-doce *uh ehr•vuh thaus*	aniseed
as ervilhas *uhz eer•vee•lyuhz*	peas
escalfado *ee•skahl•fah•thoo*	poached
o espadarte *oo ee•spah•dahr•teh*	swordfish
o espaquete *oo ee•spah•geht*	spaghetti
os espinafres *ooz ee•spee•nah•frehz*	spinach
estufado *ee•stoo•fah•thoo*	braised
o esturjão *oo ee•stoor•zsohm*	sturgeon
o faisão *oo feye•zohm*	pheasant
a farinha *uh fuh•ree•nyuh*	flour
a farofa *uh fuh•rau•fuh*	cassava flour
as favas *uhz fah•vuhz*	broad beans
o feijão *oo fay•zsohm*	bean
o feijão branco *oo fay•zsohm bruhn•koo*	navy bean
o feijão catarino *oo fay•zsohm kuh•tuh•ree•noo*	pink bean
o feijão encarnado *oo fay•zsohm eng•kuhrr•nah•thoo*	red bean
o feijão frade *oo fay•zsohm frahd*	black-eyed bean
o feijão guisado [ensopado] *oo fay•zsohm gee•sah•thoo [een•soo•pah•doo]*	beans with bacon in tomato sauce

o feijão preto *oo fay•zsohm preh•too* black bean
o feijão tropeiro *oo fay•zsohm trau•pay•roo* black beans fried with jerky
o feijão verde *oo fay•zsohm vehrd* green beans
o fiambre *oo fee•uhm•breh* boiled ham
o fígado *oo fee•guh•doo* liver
o figo *oo fee•goo* fig
o filé *oo fee•leh* steak
o filete *oo fee•leht* fillet of fish
o folhado *oo foo•lyah•thoo* sweet puff-pastry
as filhós *uhz fee•lyawz* fritters
a framboesa *uh fruhm•boo•eh•zuh* raspberry
o frango *oo fruhn•goo* chicken
o frango assado *oo fruhn•goo uh•sah•thoo* roast chicken
a fritada de peixe *uh free•tah•duh deh paysh* deep-fried fish
a fruta *uh froo•tuh* fruit
a fruta do conde *uh froo•tuh thoo kaum•deh* custard apple
a fruta em calda *uh froo•tuh eng kahl•duh* fruit in syrup
os frutos do mar *ooz froo•tuhz thoo mahr* seafood
a fubá *uh foo•bah* corn flour
a galantina *uh guh•luhn•tee•nuh* pressed meat in gelatin
o galão *oo guh•lohm* weak milky coffee
a galinha *uh guh•lee•nyuh* stewing chicken
a galinhola *uh guh•lee•nyaw•luh* woodcock
o ganso *oo guhn•soo* goose
a garoupa *uh guh•rauoo•puh* large grouper (fish)
a garrafa *uh guh•rrah•fuh* bottle
a gasosa *uh guh•zaw•zuh* lemonade
o gaspacho *oo guhz•pah•shoo* chilled soup
a gelatina *uh zseh•luh•tee•nuh* jelly
a geleia *uh zseh•lay•uh* jelly
o gelo *oo zseh•loo* ice

o gengibre *oo zsehn•zsee•breh* ginger
a goiaba *uh zsoy•ah•buh* guava
a goiabada *uh zsoy•uh•bah•duh* thick paste made of guava
o gombo *oo gaum•boo* okra
os grelos *ooz greh•looz* turnip sprouts
a groselha *uh groo•zeh•lyuh* red currant
o guisado *oo gee•zah•thoo* stew
a hortaliça *uh awr•tuh•lee•suh* fresh vegetables
a hortelã *uh awr•teh•luh* mint
o inhame *oo ee•nuhm* yam
o iogurte *oo yaw•goort* yogurt
a isca de peixe *uh ees•kuh deh paysh* fried small fish
as iscas *uhz ees•kuhz* sliced liver
a jabuticaba *uh juh•boo•tee•cah•buh* type of cherry
a jardineira *uh zsuhr•dee•nay•ruh* mixed vegetables
o javali *oo zsuh•vah•li* wild boar
o kibe *oo keeb* meat and bulgur croquette
o kiwi *oo kee•vee* kiwi
a lagosta *uh lah•gau•stuh* lobster
o lagostim *oo luh•gau•steeng* crayfish
lagostim do-rio *luh•gau•steeng doo ree•oo* fresh-water crayfish
a lampreia *uh luhm•pray•uh* lamprey
a laranja *uh luh•ruhn•zsuh* orange
a laranjada *uh luh•ruhn•zsah•thuh* orange soda
a lebre *uh leh•breh* hare
os legumes *ooz leh•goomz* vegetables
o leite *oo layt* milk
o leite de coco *oo layt deh kau•koo* coconut milk
o leitão *oo lay•tohm* suckling pig
as lentilhas *uhz lehn•tee•lyuhz* lentils
a lima *uh lee•muh* lime

o limão *oo lee•mohm*	lemon
o limão verde *oo lee•mohm vehrd*	lime
a língua *uh leen•gwuh*	tongue
o linguado *oo leen•gwah•doo*	sole
a linguíça *uh leen•gwee•suh*	thin sausage
o lombo *oo laum•boo*	loin
o louro *oo lau•roo*	bay leaf
a lula *uh loo•luh*	squid
a maçã *uh muh•suh*	apple
o macarrão *oo muh•kuh•rrohm*	macaroni
a macaxeira *uh muh•kuh•shay•ruh*	cassava root
maduro *muh•thoo•roo*	ripe
a maionese *uh meye•aw•nehz*	mayonnaise
a malagueta *uh muh•luh•geh•tuh*	hot pepper
as malsadas *uhz mahl•sah•duhz*	fried dough
o mamão *oo muh•mohm*	papaya
a mandioca *uh muhn•dee•aw•kuh*	cassava root
a manga *uh muhn•guh*	mango
o manjericão *oo muhn•zsehr•ee•kohm*	basil
a manteiga *uh muhn•tay•guh*	butter
o maracujá *oo muh•ruh•koo•zsah*	passion fruit
os mariscos *ooz muh•rees•kooz*	seafood
a marmelada *uh muhr•meh•lah•duh*	thick quince paste
a massa *uh mah•suh*	pasta; dough; pastry
o marzipã *oo marh•zee•pahn*	marzipan
o mate *oo maht*	tea with maté leaf
o medalhão *oo meh•deh•lyohm*	tenderloin steak
o medronho *oo meh•drau•nyoo*	arbutus berry (small strawberry-like fruit)
o mel *oo mehl*	honey
a melancia *uh muh•luhn•see•uh*	watermelon

o melão *oo meh•lohm*	melon
o melão com presunto *oo meh•lohm kaumpreh•zoon•too*	melon with ham
o mero *oo meh•roo*	red grouper (fish)
a mexerica *uh meh•sheh•ree•kuh*	tangerine
os mexilhões *ooz meh•shee•lyoings*	mussels
a sopa de bacalhau *uh saw•puh deh buh•kuh•lyahoo*	dried cod soup
o milho *oo mee•lyoo*	sweet corn
o milkshake *oo milk•shake*	milk shake
os miolos *ooz mee•aw•looz*	brains
o misto quente *oo mee•stoo kehnt*	ham-and-cheese toasted sandwich
o morango *oo moo•ruhn•goo*	strawberry
a morcela *uh moor•seh•luh*	blood sausage [black pudding]
a mortadela *uh moor•tuh•deh•luh*	mortadella
a mostarda *uh moo•stahr•duh*	mustard
a mousse de chocolate *uh moo•seh deh shoo•koo•laht*	chocolate pudding
a mousse de maracujá *uh moo•seh deh muh•ruh•koo•zsah*	passion fruit mousse
as nabiças *uhz nuh•bee•suhz*	turnip greens
os nabos *ooz nah•booz*	turnips
o creme *oo krehm*	fresh cream
a creme batido *uh krehm buh•tee•duh*	whipped cream
(ao) natural *(ahoo) nuh•too•rahl*	plain
as nêsperas *uhz neh•speh•ruhz*	loquat (fruit)
no forno *noo faurr•noo*	baked
a noz *uh nawz*	nut
a noz moscada *uh nawz moo•skah•thuh*	nutmeg

o óleo *oo aw•lee•oo*	oil
o óleo de amendoim *oo aw•lee•oo deh uh•mehn•doo•eeng*	peanut oil
a omelete *uh aw•meh•leht*	omelet
o orégano *oo aw•re•ga•noom*	oregano
o osso *oo au•soo*	bone
a ostra *uh aw•struh*	oyster
o ovo *oo aw•voo*	egg
os ovos cozidos *ooz aw•vooz koo•zee•thooz*	boiled eggs
os ovos escalfados *ooz aw•vooz ees•kahl•fah•thooz*	poached eggs
os ovos estrelados [fritos] *ooz aw•vooz ees•truh•lah•dooz [free•tooz]*	fried eggs
os ovos mexidos *ooz aw•vooz meh•shee•dooz*	scrambled eggs
os ovos quentes *ooz aw•vooz kehntz*	soft-boiled eggs
o palmito *oo pahl•mee•too*	palmhearts
a panqueca *uh puhn•keh•kuh*	pancake
o pão (escuro/integral) *oo pohm (ees•koo•roo/een•teh•grahl)*	bread (brown/whole wheat)
o pão de centeio *oo pohm deh sehn•tay•oo*	rye bread
o pão-de-ló *oo pohm•deh•law*	coffee cake
o pãozinho *oo pohm•zee•nyoo*	bread roll
o pargo *oo pahr•goo*	bream (fish)
as passas (de uva) *uhz pah•suhz (deh oo•vuh)*	raisin
passado *puh•sah•thoo*	cooked (meat, etc.)
o pastel *oo puhs•tehl*	small pie
o pato *oo pah•too*	duck
o pé de moleque *oo peh deh maw•leh•keh*	peanut brittle
o peito de galinha *oo pay•too deh guh•lee•nyuh*	chicken breast

o peixe *oo paysh* — fish
o peixe-agulha *oo paysh•uh•goo•lya* — garfish
o peixe-espada *oo paysh ees•pah•duh* — swordfish
o pepino *oo peh•pee•noo* — cucumber
o pepino em conserva *oo peh•pee•noo em kaum•sehr•vuh* — pickle [gherkin]
a pêra *uh peh•ruh* — pear
a perca *uh pehr•kuh* — perch
a perdiz *uh pehr•deez* — partridge
a perna de galinha *uh pehrr•nuh deh guh•lee•nyuh* — chicken leg
o pernil *oo perr•neel* — ham
o pero *oo peh•rau* — variety of apple
o peru *oo peh•roo* — turkey
os pés de porco *ooz pehz deh paur•koo* — pig's feet [trotters]
a pescada *uh pehz•kah•thuh* — whiting
o pêssego *oo peh•suh•goo* — peach
os petiscos *ooz peh•tees•kooz* — appetizers [starters]
a pevide *uh peh•veed* — salted pumpkin seed
a picanha desfiada *uh pee•kuh•nyuh dehs•fee•ah•thuh* — charcoal-grilled meat

os picles *ooz pee•kehlz*	pickled vegetables
a pimenta *uh pee•mehn•tuh*	pepper
os pimentões assados *ooz pee•mehn•tooz uh•sah•dooz*	roasted peppers
o pinhão *oo pee•nyohm*	nut
a pinhoada *uh pee•nyoo•ah•duh*	pine nut brittle
o pipis *oo pee•peez*	spicy giblet stew
o pirarucu *oo pee•ruh•roo•koo*	type of fish
o piri-piri *oo pee•ree pee•ree*	seasoning of hot chili pepper and olive oil
o polvo *oo paul•voo*	octopus
o pombo *oo paum•boo*	pigeon
o porco *oo paur•koo*	pork
a posta *uh paws•tuh*	slice of fish or meat
o presunto *oo preh•zoon•too*	cured ham
o presunto cru *oo preh•zoon•too kroo*	dried ham
o pudim *oo poo•deeng*	caramel custard
o puré de batatas *oo poo•reh deh buh•tah•tuhz*	mashed potatoes
a queijada *uh kay•zsah•duh*	small cottage-cheese tart
o queijinho do céu *oo kay•zsee•nyoo doo sehoo*	marzipan balls rolled in sugar
o queijo *oo kay•zsoo*	cheese
o quiabo *oo kee•ah•boo*	okra
o quindim *oo keeng•deeng*	pudding made with coconut and egg yolks
a rabanada *uh ruh•buh•nah•duh*	French toast
o rabanete *oo ruh•buh•neht*	radish
a raia *uh reye•uh*	skate (fish)
a rainha-cláudia *uh ray•ee•nyuh klaw•dee•uh*	greengage plum
recheado *reh•shee•ah•thoo*	stuffed

o recheio *oo re•shay•oo*	stuffing
o refogado *oo reh•foo•gah•thoo*	onions fried in olive oil
o refrigerante *oo reh•free•zsay•rahnt*	soft drink
o repolho *oo rreh•pau•lyoo*	cabbage
o requeijão *oo rre•kay•zsohm*	curd cheese
o rim *oo rreeng*	kidney
o robalo *oo rraw•buh•loo*	sea bass
o rodízio *oo rroo•dee•zee•oo*	selection of chargrilled meats
a romã *uh rrau•muh*	pomegranate
a rosca *uh rraus•kuh*	ring-shaped white bread
o rosmaninho *oo rrooz•muh•neeng•nyoo*	rosemary
o ruivo *oo rroo•ee•voo*	red gurnard (fish)
o sal *oo sahl*	salt
a salada *uh suh•lah•duh*	salad
a salada de alface/escarola *uh suh•lah•duh deh ahl•fah•seh/ees•kuh•raw•luh*	green salad
a salada de agrião *uh suh•lah•duh deh uh•gree•ohm*	watercress salad
a salada mista *uh suh•lah•duh mees•tuh*	tomato and lettuce salad
salgado *sahl•gah•thoo*	salted
o salmão (defumado) *oo suh•mohm (deh•foo•mah•do)*	(smoked) salmon
o salmonete *oo sahl•moo•neht*	red mullet
a salsa *uh sahl•suh*	parsley
a salsicha *uh sahl•see•shuh*	sausage
salteado *sahl•tee•ah•thoo*	sautéed
a sálvia *uh sahl•vee•uh*	sage
as sandes *uhz suhndz*	sandwich
o sanduíche *oo suhn•doo•eesh*	sandwich
a santola *uh suhn•taw•luh*	spider-crab
o sarapatel *oo suh•ruh•puh•tehl*	pork or mutton stew

a sarda *uh sahr•thuh* mackerel
as sardinhas *uhz suhr•dee•nyuhz* sardines
o sável *oo sah•vehl* shad (herring-like fish)
seco *seh•koo* dry
a sêmola *uh seh•moo•luh* semolina
o suflê de canela *oo soo•flay duh cuh•neh•lah* cinnamon soufflé
a sidra *uh see•druh* cider
o siri *oo see•ree* crab
as sobremesas *uhz sau•breh•meh•zuhz* dessert
a solha *uh sau•lyuh* plaice (fish)
o sonho *oo sau•nyoo* type of doughnut
a sopa *uh sau•puh* soup
o sorvete *oo sawr•veht* ice cream
o suco *oo soo•koo* fruit juice
o sururu *oo soo•roo•roo* type of cockle
o suspiro *oo soo•spee•roo* meringue
a taínha *uh tah•ee•nyuh* gray mullet (fish)
a tâmara *uh tuh•muh•ruh* date
a tangerina *uh tuhn•zsuh•ree•nuh* tangerine
a torta de amêndoa *uh tohr•tah de uh•mehn•doo•uh* almond tart
o tempero *oo tehm•peh•roo* seasoning
tenro *tehn•rroo* tender
o tomate *oo too•maht* tomato
o tomilho *oo too•mee•lyoo* thyme
a toranja *uh tau•ruhn•zsuh* grapefruit
as torradas *uhz too•rrah•duhz* toast
o torrão de ovos *oo too•rrohm deh aw•vooz* marzipan candy
a tosta *uh taw•stuh* toasted sandwich
o toucinho *oo tau•see•nyoo* bacon
o tremoço *oo treh•maw•soo* salted lupin bean

a trufa *uh troo•fuh* truffle
a truta *uh troo•tuh* trout
o tucupi *oo too•koo•pee* cassava juice
o tutano *oo too•tuh•noo* marrow
o umbu *oo oom•boo* tropical fruit
as uvas *uhz oo•vuhz* grapes
as vagens *uhz vah•gehnz* green beans
variado *vuh•ree•ah•thoo* assorted
o veado *oo vee•ah•thoo* venison
os vegetais variados *ooz veh•zseh•teyez vuh•ree•ah•thooz* mixed vegetables
a vieira *uh vee•ay•ruh* scallop
o vinagre *oo vee•nah•greh* vinegar
a vitela *uh vee•tehl•uh* veal

People

Conversation

ESSENTIAL

Hello.	**Oi.** *au•hee*
How are you?	**Tudo bem?** *Too•duh beng*
Fine, thanks.	**Bem, obrigado** *m* **/obrigada** *f.* *behm aw•bree•gah•doo/aw•bree•gah•duh*
Excuse me!	**Desculpe!** *dehz•kool•peh*
Do you speak English?	**Fala inglês?** *fah•luh eeng•lehz*
What's your name?	**Como se chama?** *kau•moo seh shuh•muh*
My name is…	**Meu nome é…** *mehoo naum•ee eh…*
Nice to meet you.	**Muito prazer.** *mooee•too pruh•zehr*
Where are you from?	**De onde é?** *deh aund eh*
I'm from the U.S./U.K.	**Sou dos Estados Unidos/da Inglaterra.** *soh dooz ee•stah•dooz oo•nee•dooz/* *duh eeng•luh•teh•rruh*
What do you do?	**O que é que faz?** *oo kee eh keh fahz*
I work for…	**Trabalho para…** *truh•bah•lyoo puh•ruh…*
I'm a student.	**Sou estudante.** *sauoo ee•stoo•duhnt*
I'm retired.	**Sou aposentado** *m* **/aposentada** *f.* *soh uh•poo•zehn•tah•doo/uh•poo•zehn•tah•duh*
Do you like…?	**Gosta de…?** *gaw•stuh deh…*
Goodbye.	**Tchau.** *chah•oo*
See you later.	**Até mais tarde.** *uh•teh meyez tahrd*

Você is predominantly used for "you" when talking to anyone, regardless of age or class. **Você(s)** takes either the third person singular or the third person plural of the verb depending on whether you're referring to one person (**você**) or more than one person (**vocês**).

Language Difficulties

Do you speak English?	**Fala inglês?** *fah•luh eeng•lehz*
Does anyone here speak English?	**Alguém que fale inglês?** *ahl•gehng keh fah•leh eeng•lehz*
I don't speak (much) Portuguese.	**Não falo (muito) português.** *nohm fah•loo (mooee•too) poor•too•gehz*
Could you speak more slowly?	**Pode falar mais devagar?** *pawd fuh•lahr meyez deh•vuh•gahr*
Could you repeat that?	**Pode repetir?** *pawd reh•peh•teer*
Excuse me? [Pardon?]	**Desculpe?** *dehz•kool•peh*
What was that?	**Como disse?** *kau•moo dee•seh*
Could you spell it?	**Pode soletrar?** *pawd sau•leh•trahr*
Please write it down.	**Escreva, por favor.** *ee•screhv poor fuh•vaur*
Can you translate this for me?	**Pode traduzir isto?** *pawd truh•doo•zeer ee•stoo*
What does this/that mean?	**O que significa isto/aquilo?** *oo keh sehg•nee•fee•kuh ee•stoo/uh•kee•loo*
I understand.	**Entendo.** *ehn•tehn•doo*
I don't understand.	**Não entendo.** *nohm ehn•tehn•doo*
Do you understand?	**Entende?** *ehn•tehn•deh*

For Communications, see page 52.

YOU MAY HEAR...

Falo só um pouco de Inglês. *fah•loo saw oong pau•koo deh eeng•lehz*	I only speak a little English.
Nao falo Inglês. *nohm fah•loo eeng•lehz*	I don't speak English.

Making Friends

Hello.	**Oi.** *Au•hee*
Good morning.	**Bom dia.** *bong dee•uh*
Good afternoon.	**Boa tarde.** *baw•uh tahrd*
Good evening.	**Boa noite.** *baw•uh noyt*
My name is...	**Meu nome é...** *mehoo naum•ee eh...*
What's your name?	**Como se chama?** *kau•moo seh shuh•muh*
I'd like to introduce you to...	**Gostaria de te apresentar ao/à...** *goo•stuh•ree•uh deh the uh•preh•sehn•tahr ahoo/ah...*
Nice to meet you.	**Muito prazer.** *mooee•too preh•zehr*
How are you?	**Como está?** *kau•moo ee•stah*
Fine, thanks.	**Bem, obrigado** *m* **/obrigada** *f***.** *beng aw•bree•gah•doo/aw•bree•gah•duh*
And you?	**E o senhor** *m* **/a senhora** *f***?** *ee oo seh•nyaur/uh seh•nyau•ruh*

In Brazil, a standard greeting is a handshake accompanied by direct eye contact and the appropriate greeting for the time of day. Once a closer relationship has developed, greetings become more personal: men may greet each other with a hug, and women kiss each other twice on the cheek starting on the right-hand side. Brazilians often use a first name with a title of respect: **Senhor** for men, **Senhora** or **Dona** for women. Wait until invited before moving to a first-name basis.

Travel Talk

I'm here...	**Estou aqui...** *ee•stawoo uh•kee...*
on business	**a negócios** *ah neh•gaw•see•yooz*
on vacation [holiday]	**de férias** *deh feh•ree•uhz*
studying	**estudando** *ee•stoo•duhn•doo*
I'm staying for...	**Fico por...** *fee•koo poor...*
I've been here...	**Eu já estive aqui...** *ehoo zsah ee•stee•veh uh•kee...*
a day	**um dia** *oong dee•uh*
a week	**uma semana** *oo•muh seh•muh•nuh*
a month	**um mês** *oong mehz*
Where are you from?	**De onde é?** *deh aund eh*
I'm from...	**Sou...** *sawoo...*

For Numbers, see page 173.

Personal

Who are you with?	**Com quem está?** *kaun keng ee•stah*
I'm on my own.	**Estou sozinho** *m* **/sozinha** *f*. *ee•stawoo saw•zee•nyoo/saw•zee•nyuh*
I'm with my...	**Estou com o meu** *m* **/a minha** *f*... *ee•stawoo kaum oo mehoo/uh mee•nyuh...*

husband/wife	**marido/mulher** *muh•ree•thoo/moo•lyehr*
boyfriend/girlfriend	**namorado/namorada** *nuh•moo•rah•thoo/ nuh•moo•rah•thuh*
friend(s)	**amigo(s)** *m* **/amiga(s)** *f uh•mee•goo(z)/ uh•mee•guh(z)*
colleague(s)	**colega(s)** *koo•leh•guh(z)*
When's your birthday?	**Quando faz aniversário?** *kwuhn•doo fahz uh•ni•vehr•sah•ree•oo*
How old are you?	**Quantos anos tem?** *kwuhn•tooz uh•noos teng*
I'm…	**Eu tenho…** *ehoo teh•nyoo…*
Are you married?	**É casado** *m* **/casada** *f***?** *eh kuh•zah•doo/kuh•zah•duh*
I'm…	**Sou…/Estou…** *sawoo/ee•stawoo…*
single	**solteiro** *m* **/solteira** *f saul•tay•roo/(saul•tay•ruh)*
in a relationship	**num relacionamento** *noong reh•luh•see•oo•nuh•mehn•too*
I'm…	**Sou…/Estou…** *sawoo/ee•stawoo…*
engaged	**comprometido** *kaum•proo•meh•tee•doo*
married	**casado** *m* **/casada** *f kuh•zah•doo/kuh•zah•duh*
divorced	**divorciado** *m* **/divorciada** *f dee•voor•see•ah•doo/ dee•voor•see•ah•duh*
separated	**separado** *m* **/separada** *f seh•puh•rah•doo/ seh•puh•rah•duh*
I'm widowed.	**Sou viúvo** *m* **/viúva** *f***.** *sau vee•oo•voo/vee•oo•vuh*
Do you have children/ grandchildren?	**Tem filhos/netos?** *teng fee•lyooz/neh•tooz*

Work & School

What do you do?	**O que é que faz?** *oo kee eh keh fahz*
What are you studying?	**O que é que está estudando?** *oo kee eh keh ee•stah ee•stoo•duhn•doo*

I'm studying...	**Estudo...** *ee•stoo•doo...*
I work full time/ part time.	**Trabalho tempo período/meio tempo.** *truh•bah•lyoo tehm•poo puh•ree•ooduh/may•oo tehm•poo*
I'm between jobs.	**Estou entre empregos.** *ee•stawoo ehn•treh ehng•preh•gooz*
I'm unemployed.	**Estou desempregado.** *ee•stawoo deh•zehm•preh•gah•doo.*
I work at home.	**Trabalho em casa.** *truh•bah•lyoo eng kah•zuh*
Who do you work for?	**Para quem trabalha?** *puh•ruh keng truh•bah•lyuh*
I work for...	**Trabalho para...** *truh•bah•lyoo puh•ruh...*
Here's my business card.	**Aqui está meu cartão.** *uh•kee ee•stah mehoo kuhr•tohm*

Weather

What's the weather forecast?	**Quais são as previsões do tempo?** *kweyez sohm uhz preh•vee•zoings thoo tehm•poo*
What beautiful/ terrible weather!	**Que tempo tão lindo/ruim!** *keh tehm•poo tohm leen•doo/rroo•eeng*
It's cool/warm.	**Está fresco/calor.** *ee•stah frehs•koo/kuh•laur*
It's hot/cold.	**Está calor/frio.** *ee•stah kuh•laur/free-oo.*
It's rainy/sunny.	**Está um dia de chuva/sol.** *ee•stah oong dee•uh deh shoo•vuh/sawl*
It's snowy/icy.	**Está um dia de neve/com gelo.** *ee•stah oong dee•uh deh nehv/kaum zseh•loo*
Do I need a jacket/ an umbrella?	**Preciso de um casaco/guarda-chuva?** *preh•see•zoo deh oong kuh•zah•koo/goo•ahr•dah shoo•vuh*

Romance

ESSENTIAL

Would you like to go out for a drink/dinner?	**Quer tomar uma bebida/comer fora?** *kehr too•mahr oo•muh beh•bee•thuh/koo•mehr faw•ruh*
What are your plans for tonight/tomorrow?	**Quais são os seus planos para hoje à noite/ amanhã?** *kweyez sohm ooz sehooz pluh•nooz puh•ruh auzseh ah noyt/uh•muh•nyuh*
Can I have your number?	**Qual o seu número de telefone?** *Kwal oo seoh noo•meh•roo deh tehl•fawn*
Can I join you?	**Posso te acompanhar?** *paw•soo teh uh•kaum•puh•nyahr*
Can I buy you a drink?	**O que quer beber?** *oo keh kehr beh•behr*
I like you.	**Gosto de você.** *gawzh•too deh voh•seh*
I love you.	**Te amo.** *teh uh•moo*

The Dating Game

Would you like to go out for...?	**Quer sair para...?** *kehr seh•eer puh•ruh...*
coffee	**um café** *oong kuh•feh*
a drink	**uma bebida** *oo•muh beh•bee•thuh*
dinner	**jantar** *zsuhn•tahr*
What are your plans for...?	**Quais são os seus planos para...?** *kweyez sohm ooz sehooz pluh•nooz puh•ruh...*
tonight	**hoje à noite** *auzseh ah noyt*
tomorrow	**amanhã** *uh•muh•nyuh*
this weekend	**este fim de semana** *ehst feeng deh seh•muh•nuh*

Where would you like to go?	**Onde quer ir?** *aund kehr eer*
I'd like to go to…	**Quero ir à…** *keh•roo eer ah…*
Do you like…?	**Gosta de…?** *gaw•stuh deh…*
Can I have your number/e-mail?	**Podes me dar o seu número de telefone/ e-mail?** *pawd•ehz meh dahr oo sehoo noo•meh•roo deh tehl•fawn /ee•mehl*
Are you on Facebook/ Twitter?	**Está no Facebook/Twitter?** *ee•stah noo facebook/ twitter*
Can I join you?	**Posso te acompanhar?** *paw•soo teh uh•kaum•puh•nyahr*
You look great!	**Está linda!** *ee•stah leen•duh*
Let's go somewhere quieter.	**Vamos para um lugar mais sossegado.** *vuh•mooz puh•ruh oong loo•gahr meyez soo•seh•gah•thoo*

For Communications, see page 52.

Accepting & Rejecting

I'd love to.	**Adoraria ir.** *uh•doo•ruh•ree•uh eer*
Where should we meet?	**Onde vamos nos encontrar?** *aund vuh•mooz nooz ehng•kaun•trahr*

I'll meet you at the bar/ your hotel.	**Vou te encontrar no bar/hotel.** *vauoo tee ehn•kaun•trahr noo bahr/aw•tehl*
I'll come by at…	**Eu passo por lá às…** *ehoo pah•soo poor lah ahz…*
What's your address?	**Qual é o suo endereço?** *kwahl eh uh soo•uh ehn•deh•reh•soo*
I'm busy.	**Mas tenho muito que fazer.** *muhz teh•nyoo mooee•too keh fuh•zehr*
I'm not interested.	**Não estou interessado *m* /interessada *f*.** *nohm ee•stawoo een•treh•sah•thoo/een•treh•sah•thuh*
Leave me alone.	**Me deixe em paz.** *meh day•sheh eng pahz*
Stop bothering me!	**Páre!** *pah•reeee*

Getting Intimate

Can I hug/kiss you?	**Posso te dar um abraço/beijo?** *paw•soo teh dahr oong uh•brah•soo/bay•zsoo*
Yes.	**Sim.** *seeng*
No.	**Não.** *nohm*
Stop!	**Pára!** *pah•ruh*
I love you.	**Te amo.** *teh uh•moo*

Sexual Preferences

Are you gay?	**Você é homossexual?** *Voh•seh eh aw•maw•sehk•soo•ahl*
I'm…	**Sou…** *sauoo…*
heterosexual	**heterossexual** *eh•teh•raw•sehk•soo•ahl*
homosexual	**homossexual** *aw•maw•sehk•soo•ahl*
bisexual	**bissexual** *bee•sehk•soo•ahl*
Do you like men/ women?	**Gosta de homens/mulheres?** *gaw•stuh deh aw•mengz/moo•lyehrz*

For Grammar, see page 169.

Leisure Time

Sightseeing

ESSENTIAL

Where's the tourist office?	**Onde é o posto de informações turísticas?** *aund eh oo pau•stoo deh een•foor•muh•soings too•ree•stee•kuhz*
What are the main points of interest?	**O que há de mais interessante para se ver?** *oo kee ah deh meyez een•tehr•reh•suhnt puh•ruh seh vehr*
Do you have tours in English?	**Tem excursões em inglês?** *teng ee•skoor•soings eng eng•lehz*
Can I have a map/guide?	**Pode me dar um mapa/guia?** *pawd meh dahr oong mah•puh/ gee•uh*

Tourist Information

Do you have any information on...?	**Tem informação sobre...?** *teng een•foor•muh•sohm sau•breh...*
Can you recommend...?	**Pode recomendar...?** *pawd reh•koo•mehn•dahr...*
a boat trip	**uma excursão de barco** *oo•muh ee•skoor•sohm deh bahr•koo*
an excursion	**uma excursão** *oo•muh ee•skoor•sohm*
a sightseeing tour	**um circuito turístico** *oong seer•koo•ee•too too•ree•stee•koo*

For Disabled Travelers, see page 153.

Town maps and brochures on main tourist attractions are available at airports and from tourist information centers. Ask at your hotel or check online to find the nearest office.

On Tour

I'd like to go on the tour to...	**Gostaria de ir na excursão para...** *goo•stuh•ree•uh deh eer nuh ee•skoor•sohm puh•ruh...*
When's the next tour?	**Quando é a próxima excursão?** *kwuhn•doo eh uh praw•see•muh ee•skoor•sohm*
Are there tours in English?	**Há excursões em inglês?** *ah ee•skoor•soings eng eeng•lehz*
Is there an English-speaking guide/audio guide?	**Há algum guia que fale inglês/uma gravação da visita guiada em inglês?** *ah ahl•goong gee•uh keh fah•leh eeng•lehz/oo•muh gruh•vuh•sohm deh vee•zee•tuh gee•ah•duh eng eeng•lehz*
What time do we leave/return?	**Quando saímos/regressemos?** *kwuhn•doo suh•eemooz/reh•greh•seh•mooz*
We'd like to see...	**Gostaríamos de ver...** *goo•stuh•ree•uh•mooz deh vehr...*
Can we stop here...?	**Podemos parar aqui...?** *poo•deh•mooz puh•rahr uh•kee...*
to take photographs	**para tirar fotografias** *puh•ruh tee•rahr foo•too•gruh•fee•uhz*
to buy souvenirs	**para comprar lembranças** *puh•ruh kaum•prahr leng•bruhn•suhz*

to use the restrooms [toilets]	**para usar os banheiros** *puh•ruh oo•zahr ooz buh•nyay•rooz*
Is there access for the disabled?	**Há algum acesso para os deficientes?** *ah ahl•goong uh•seh•soo puh•ruh ooz deh•fee•see•ehntz*

For Tickets, see page 20.

Seeing the Sights

Where is/are...?	**Onde é/são...?** *aund eh/sohm...*
the battleground	**o campo de batalha** *oo kuhm•poo deh buh•tah•lyuh*
the botanical garden	**o jardim botânico** *oo zsuhr•deeng boo•tuh•nee•koo*
the castle	**o castelo** *oo kuhz•teh•loo*
the downtown area	**o centro da cidade** *oo sehn•troo duh see•dahd*
the fountain	**a fonte** *uh faun•teh*
the library	**a biblioteca** *uh bee•blee•aw•teh•kuh*
the market	**o mercado** *oo mehr•kah•doo*
the museum	**o museu** *oo moo•zehoo*
the old town	**a parte velha da cidade** *uh pahrt veh•lyuh duh see•dahd*
the palace	**o palácio** *oo puh•lah•see•yoo*
the park	**o parque** *oo pahr•keh*
the ruins	**as ruínas** *uhz roo•een•uhz*
the shopping area	**a área comercial** *uh ah•ree•uh koo•mehr•see•ahl*
the town square	**a praça central** *uh prah•suh sehn•trahl*
Can you show me on the map?	**Pode indicar no mapa?** *pawd een•dee•kahr noo mah•puh*
It's...	**É...** *eh...*
amazing	**espantoso** *ee•spuhn•tau•zoo*
beautiful	**lindo** *leen•doo*
boring	**aborrecido** *uh•boo•rreh•see•thoo*

interesting	**interessante** *een•teh•reh•suhnt*
magnificent	**magnífico** *mahg•nee•fee•koo*
romantic	**romântico** *roo•muhn•tee•koo*
strange	**estranho** *ee•struh•nyoo*
stunning	**estupendo** *ee•stoo•pehn•doo*
terrible	**horrível** *aw•rree•vehl*
ugly	**feio** *fay•oo*
I (don't) like any of it.	**(Não) gosto de tudo.** *(nohm) gaw•stoo deh too•thoo*

For Asking Directions, see page 36.

Religious Sites

Where's...?	**Onde é...?** *aund eh...*
the cathedral	**a catedral** *uh keh•teh•drahl*
the Catholic/ Protestant church	**a igreja católica/protestante** *uh ee•gray•zsuh kuh•taw•lee•kuh/praw•tee•stuhnt*
the mosque	**a mesquita** *uh mehz•kee•tuh*
Where's...?	**Onde é...?** *aund eh...*
the shrine	**o relicário** *oo reh•lee•kah•ree•oo*
the synagogue	**a sinagoga** *uh seen•uh•gaw•guh*
the temple	**o templo** *oo tehm•ploo*
What time is mass/ the service?	**A que horas é a missa/o culto?** *uh kee aw•ruhz eh uh mee•suh/oo kool•too*

Shopping

ESSENTIAL

Where is the market/ mall [shopping?	**Onde é o mercado/o centro comercial?** *aund eh oo mehr•kah•thoo/oo sehn•troo koo•mehr•see•ahl*
I'm just looking.	**Estou só vendo.** *ee•stawoo saw vehn•doo*
Can you help me?	**Pode me ajudar?** *pawd meh uh•zsoo•dahr*
I'm being helped.	**Alguém está me ajudando.** *ahl•gehng ee•stah uh meh uh•zsoo•dahd•doh*
How much is it?	**Quanto é?** *kwuhn•too eh*
That one, please.	**Aquele** *m* **/Aquela** *f*, **por favor.** *uh•kehl/uh•keh•luh poor fuh•vaur*
That's all, thanks.	**Étudo, obrigado** *m* **/obrigada** *f*. *eh too•doo aw•bree•gah•doo/aw•bree•gah•thuh*
Where can I pay?	**Onde pago?** *aund pah•goo*
I'll pay in cash/ by credit card.	**Pago com dinheiro/com o cartão de crédito.** *pah•goo kaum dee•nyay•roo/kaum oo kuhr•tohm deh kreh•dee•too*
A receipt, please.	**Um recibo, por favor.** *oong reh•see•boo poor fuh•vaur*

Some particularly good, value-for-money items to look out for in Brazil include: gemstones and jewelry, leather goods such as sandals, bags, belts and wallets, wooden objects such as salad bowls and trays and woodcarvings, Brazilian percussion instruments and music, lace and embroidery or beachware, religious articles and of course, coffee.

At the Shops

Where is/are...?	**Onde é/são...?** *aund eh/sohm...*
the antiques store	**a loja das antiguidades** *uh law•zsuh duhz uhn•tee•gee•dah•dehz*
the bakery	**a padaria** *uh pah•deh•ree•uh*
the bank	**o banco** *oo buhn•koo*
the bookstore	**a livraria** *uh lee•vreh•ree•uh*
the clothing store	**a loja de artigos de vestuário** *uh law•zsuh deh uhr•tee•gooz de veh•stoo•ah•ree•oo*
the delicatessen	**a loja de conveniência** *uh law•zsuh deh kohn•vuh•nee•uhn•see•ah*
the department store	**a loja de departamentos** *uh law•zsuh deh deh•puhr•tuh•mehn•tooz*
the gift shop	**a loja de recordações** *uh law•zsuh deh reh•kaur•duh•soingz*
the health food store	**a loja de produtos dietéticos** *uh law•zsuh deh proo•doo•tooz dee•eh•tee•kooz*
the jeweler	**a joalheria** *uh zsoo•uh•lyeh•ree•uh*
the liquor store [off-licence]	**a loja de vinhos** *uh law•zsuh deh vee•nyooz*
the market	**o mercado** *oo mehr•kah•doo*
the music store	**a loja de música** *uh law•zsuh deh moo•zee•cuh*
Where is/are...?	**Onde é/são...?** *aund eh/sohm...*
the pastry shop	**a confeitaria** *uh kaun•fay•tuh•ree•uh*
the pharmacy [chemist]	**a farmácia** *uh fuhr•mah•see•uh*
the produce [grocery] store	**a quitanda** *uh kee•tuhn•duh*
the shoe store	**a sapataria** *uh suh•puh•tuh•ree•uh*
the shopping mall [shopping centre]	**o centro comercial** *oo sehn•troo koo•mehr•see•ahl*

the souvenir store	**a loja de lembranças** *uh law•zsuh deh lehn•bruhn•suhz*
the supermarket	**o supermercado** *oo soo•pehr•mehr•kah•thoo*
the tobacconist	**a tabacaria** *uh tuh•bah•kuh•ree•uh*
the toy store	**a loja de brinquedos** *uh law•zsuh deh breeng•keh•dooz*

Ask an Assistant

What are the opening hours?	**Qual a hora de abertura?** *kwahl uh aw•ruh deh ah•behr•too•ruh*
Where is/are...?	**Onde é/são...?** *aund eh/sohm...*
the cashier	**a caixa** *uh keye•shuh*
the escalator	**a escada rolante** *uh ees•kah•duh roo•luhnt*
the elevator [lift]	**o elevador** *oo eh•leh•vuh•daur*
the fitting room	**os vestiários** *ooz vehs•tee•ah•ree•ooz*
the store directory [guide]	**a planta da loja** *uh pluhn•tuh duh law•zsuh*
Can you help me?	**Pode me ajudar?** *pawd meh uh•zsoo•dahr*
I'm just looking.	**Estou só vendo.** *ee•stawoo saw vehn•doo*
I'm being helped.	**Alguém está a me ajudar.** *ahl•geng ee•stah uh meh uh•zsoo•dahr*
Do you have...?	**Tem...?** *teng...*

Could you show me...? **Pode me mostrar...?** *poo•dee meh mooz•trahr...*
Can you ship it /wrap it ? **Pode despachá-lo/embrulhá-lo?** *pawd dehs•puh•shah•loo/eng•broo•lyah•loo*
How much is it? **Quanto é?** *kwuhn•too eh*
That's all, thanks. **É tudo, obrigado** *m* **/obrigada** *f.* *eh too•doo aw•bree•gah•doo/aw•bree•gah•duh*

For Clothing, see page 127.

YOU MAY HEAR...

Deseja alguma coisa? *deh•zay•zuh ahl•goo•muh koy•zuh* Would you like something?
Um momento. *oong moo•mehn•too* One moment.
O que é que deseja? *oo kee eh keh deh•zay•zsuh* What would you like?
Mais alguma coisa? *meyez ahl•goo•muh koy•zuh* Anything else?

YOU MAY SEE...

HORÁRIO DE ABERTURA opening hours
FECHADO PARA ALMOÇO closed for lunch
PROVADOR fitting room
CAIXA cashier
SÓ DINHEIRO cash only
CARTÕES DE CRÉDITO ACEITES credit cards accepted

Personal Preferences

I'd like something…	**Queria uma coisa…** *keh•ree•uh oo•muh koy•zuh…*
cheap/expensive	**barata/cara** *buh•rah•tuh/kah•ruh*
larger/smaller	**maior/menor** *meye•awr/mee•nawr*
from this region	**desta região** *dehs•tuh ree•zsee•ohm*
Around… reais.	**Cerca de… reais.** *sehr•ka deh… rree•eyez*
Is it real?	**É verdadeiro?** *eh vehr•duh•day•roo*
Could you show me this/that ?	**Podia mostrar-me este/esse?** *poo•dee•uh moos•trahr•meh ehst/ehs*
That's not quite what I want.	**Não é bem o que quero.** *nohm eh beng oo keh keh•roo*
No, I don't like it.	**Não, não gosto.** *nohm nohm gaw•stoo*
It's too expensive.	**É caro demais.** *eh kah•roo deh•meyez*
I have to think about it.	**Tenho que pensar nisto.** *tay•nyoo keh pehn•sahr nee•stoo*
I'll take it.	**Levo.** *leh•voo*

For Souvenirs see page 133.

Paying & Bargaining

How much?	**Quanto é?** *kwuhn•too eh*
I'll pay…	**Pago…** *pah•goo…*
in cash	**com dinheiro** *kaum dee•nyay•roo*
by credit card	**com o cartão de crédito** *kaum oo kuhr•tohm deh kreh•dee•too*
by traveler's check [cheque]	**com cheque** *kaum sheh•keh*
A receipt, please.	**Um recibo, por favor.** *oong reh•see•boo poor fuh•vaur*
That's too much.	**Isso é muito.** *ee•soo eh mooee•too*
I'll give you…	**Vou dar-lhe…** *vau dahr•lyeh…*
I only have… reais.	**Só tenho…reais.** *saw teh•nyoo…rree•eyez*

Is that your best price?	**É o preço melhor que me pode dar?** *eh oo preh•soo mee•lyawr keh meh pawd dahr*
Can you give me a discount?	**Pode-me dar um desconto?** *pawd•meh dahr oong dehs•kaun•too*

For Numbers, see page 173.

International credit cards are generally accepted. The most commonly used cards are Visa™, American Express®, Europay/Mastercard™, JCB and Maestro®. In some small villages and towns cash may still be the only form of currency accepted.

YOU MAY HEAR...

Como deseja pagar? *kau•moo deh•zay•zsuh puh•gahr*	How are you paying?
Esta transação não foi autorizada. *eh•stuh truhn•suh•sohm nohm foy ahoo•too•ree•zah•thuh*	This transaction was not authorized.
Não aceitamos cartões de crédito. *nohm uh•say•tuh•mooz kuhr•toings deh kreh•dee•too*	We don't accept credit cards.
Só com dinheiro, por favor. *saw kaum dee•nyay•roo poor fuh•vaur*	Cash only, please.
Não tem troco [trocado]? *nohm teng trau•koo [trau•kah•doo]*	Do you have any smaller bills?
A identificação, por favor. *uh ee•dehnt•tee•fee•kuh•sohm, poor fuh•vaur*	ID, please.

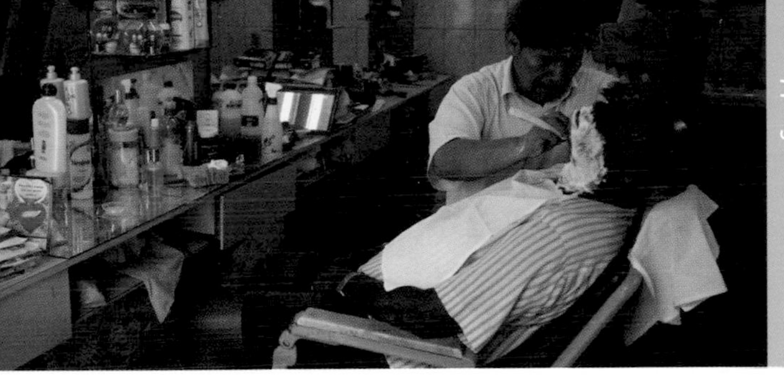

Making a Complaint

I'd like…	**Queria…** *keh•ree•uh…*
to exchange this	**trocar isto** *troo•kahr ee•stoo*
to return this	**retornar isto** *ree•tawrr•nahr ee•stoo*
a refund	**um reembolso** *oong ree•eng•baul•soo*
to see the manager	**falar com o gerente** *m* **/a gerente** *f fuh•lahr kaum oo zseh•rehnt/uh zseh•rehnt*

Services

Can you recommend…?	**Pode recomendar…?** *pawd reh•koo•mehn•dahr…*
a barber	**o cabeleireiro de homens** *oo kuh•beh•lay•ray•roo deh aw•mengs*
a dry cleaner	**a lavandaria de limpeza a seco** *uh luh•vuhn•duh•ree•uh deh leeng•peh•zuh uh seh•koo*
a hairdresser	**o cabeleireiro de senhoras** *oo kuh•beh•lay•ray•roo deh see•nyau•ruhz*
a laundromat [launderette]	**lavanderia** *uh luh•vuhn•deh•ree•uh*
a nail salon	**o salão de unhas** *oo suh•lohm deh oo•nyuhz*
a spa	**o spa** *oo spa*
a travel agency	**a agência de viagens** *uh ah•zsehn•see•uh deh vee•ah•zsengs*

Can you...this?	**Pode...isto?** *pawd...ee•stoo*
alter	**modificar** *moo•dee•fee•kahr*
clean	**limpar** *leem•parh*
mend	**consertar** *kaun•sehr•tahr*
press	**engomar** *eeng•goo•mahr*
When will it be ready?	**Quando estará pronto?** *kwuhn•doo ee•stuh•rah praun•too*

Hair & Beauty

I'd like...	**Queria...** *keh•ree•uh...*
an appointment for today/tomorrow	**marcar um horário para hoje/amanhã** *muhr•kahr oong aw•rah•ree•oo puh•ruh auzseh/uh•muh•nyuh*
some color	**alguma cor** *ahl•goo•muh kaur*
some highlights	**madeixas** *muh•day•shuhz*
my hair styled/ blow-dried	**meu cabelo penteado/seco com secador** *mehoo kuh•beh•loo pehn•tee•ah•thoo/seh•koo kaum seh•kuh•daur*
a haircut	**um corte** *oong kawrt*
a trim	**acertar as pontas [aparar]** *uh•sehr•tahr uhz paun•tuhz [uh•puh•rahr]*
Don't cut it too short.	**Não corte muito curto.** *nohm kawrt mooee•too koor•too*
Shorter here.	**Mais curto aqui.** *meyez koor•too uh•kee*
I'd like...	**Queria...** *keh•ree•uh...*
an eyebrow/ a bikini wax	**depilar as sombrancelhas/depilar para biquini** *duh•pee•lahr oo•muh seh•ruh deh sau•bruhn•seh•lyuhz/par•ah bee•kee•nee*
I'd like...	**Queria...** *keh•ree•uh...*
a facial	**uma limpeza de pele** *oo•muh leem•peh•zuh deh pehl*

a manicure/pedicure	**fazer as unhas das mãos/pés** *faz•uhr uhz oo•nyaz duhz muh•oonz/pehz*
a (sports) massage	**uma massagem (esportiva)** *oo•muh mehn•sah•zseng (ee•spawr•tee•vuh)*
Do you do…?	**Faz…?** *fahz…*
acupuncture	**acupuntura** *uh•koo•poon•too•ruh*
aromatherapy	**aromaterapia** *uh•raw•muh•teh•reh•pee•uh*
oxygen treatment	**tratamento de oxigênio** *truh•tuh•mehn•too deh awk•see•zseh•nee•oo*
Is there a sauna?	**Há sauna?** *ah sahoo•nuh*

Check with your hotel concierge for information on local spas that offer massage, acupuncture and skin treatments. These spas are most often found in large cities. The service fee is usually included in the price, but an additional 10% tip is appreciated for good service.

Antiques

How old is this?	**Qual é a data disto?** *kwahl eh uh dah•tuh dee•stoo*
Do you have anything from the…period?	**Tem alguma coisa do período…?** *teng ahl•goo•muh koy•zuh thoo peh•ree•oo•thoo…*
Do I have to fill out any forms?	**Tenho que completar algum formulário?** *teh•nyoo keh kaum•pleh•tahr ahl•goom fawr•moo•lah•ree•oo*
Is there a certificate of authenticity?	**Há um certificado de autenticidade?** *ah oong sehr•tee•fee•kah•thoo deh aw•tehn•tee•see•dahd*
Can you ship/wrap it?	**Pode enviar/embrulhar?** *pawd ehn•vee•ahr/ehm•broo•lyahr*

Clothing

I'd like... **Queria...** *keh•ree•uh...*

Can I try this on? **Posso provar isto?** *paw•soo proo•vahr ee•stoo*

It doesn't fit. **Não me serve.** *nohm meh sehrv*

It's too... **É muito...** *eh mooee•too...*

big **grande** *grawnd*

small **pequeno** *m* **/pequena** *f peh•kehn•oo/peh•kehn•uh*

short **curto** *m* **/curta** *f koor•too/koor•tuh*

long **comprido** *m* **/comprida** *f kaum•pree•doo/kaum•pree•duh*

tight/loose **justo/largo** *zsooz•too/lahr•goo*

Do you have this in size...? **Tem isto no tamanho...?** *teng ee•stoo noo tuh•muh•nyoo...*

Do you have this in a bigger/smaller size? **Tem isto num tamanho maior/menor?** *teng ee•stoo noong tuh•muh•nyoo meye•awr/mee•nor*

For Numbers, see page 173.

YOU MAY HEAR...

Isso fica bem em você. *ee•soo fee•kuh beng eng voh•seh* That looks great on you.

Como é que fica? *kau•moo eh keh fee•kuh* How does it fit?

Não temos o seu tamanho. *nohm teh•mooz oo sehoo tuh•muh•nyoo* We don't have your size.

YOU MAY SEE...

ROUPA DE HOMEM men's clothing

ROUPA DE SENHORA women's clothing

ROUPA DE CRIANÇAS children's clothing

Colors

I'd like something… **Queria algo…** *keh•ree•uh ahl•goo…*

- beige **em bege** *eng bay•zseh*
- black **em preto** *eng preh•too*
- blue **em azul** *eng uh•zool*
- brown **em marrom** *muh•rraum*
- green **em verde** *eng vehrd*
- gray **em cinza** *eng seen•zuh*
- orange **em laranja** *eng luh•ruhn•zsuh*
- pink **em cor-de-rosa** *eng kaur deh raw•zuh*
- purple **em roxo** *eng rau•shoo*
- red **em vermelho** *eng vehr•meh•lyoo*
- white **em branco** *eng bruhn•koo*
- yellow **em amarelo** *eng uh•meh•reh•loo*

Clothes & Accessories

backpack **a mochila** *uh moo•shee•luh*

belt **o cinto** *oo seen•too*

bikini **o bikini [biquini]** *oo bee•kee•nee [bee•kee•nee]*

blouse **a blusa** *uh bloo•zuh*

bra **o sutiã** *oo soo•tee•uh*

briefs [underpants] **as calcinhas** *uhz kahl•see•nyuhz*

coat **o casaco comprido** *oo kuh•zah•koo kaum•pree•thoo*

dress **o vestido** *oo vehs•tee•thoo*

hat **o chapéu** *oo shuh•pehoo*

jacket **o casaco curto** *oo kuh•zah•koo koor•too*

jeans **as calças jeans** *uhz kahl•suhz jeans*

pants [trousers] **as calças** *uhz kahl•suhz*

pantyhose [tights] **o collant** *oo koo•luhnt*

purse [handbag] **a mala de mão [bolsa]**

	uh mah•luh deh mohm [baul•sah]
raincoat	**capa de chuva** *cah•pah deh shoo•vah*
scarf	**o lenço de pescoço** *oo lehn•soo deh pehz•kau•soo*
shirt	**a camisa** *uh kuh•mee•zuh*
shorts	**os shorts** *ooz shortz*
skirt	**a saia** *uh seye•uh*
socks	**as meias curtas** *uhz may•uhz koor•tuhz*
suit	**o terno** *oo tehr•noo*
sunglasses	**os óculos de sol** *ooz aw•koo•looz deh sawl*
sweater	**o suéter** *oo sweh•tur*
sweatshirt	**o sweatshirt** *oo sweht•shurt [uh bloo•zuh deh mool•ee•tawn]*
swimming trunks	**os shorts de banho** *ooz shortz deh buh•nyoo*
swimsuit	**o maiô** *oo meye•au*
T-shirt	**a camiseta/T-shirt** *uh kuh•mee•seh•tuh/tee•shurt*
tie	**gravata** *gruh•vah•tuh*
underwear	**roupa de baixo** *rau•puh deh bah•ee•shoo*

Fabric

I'd like…	**Queria…** *keh•ree•uh…*
cotton	**algodão** *ahl•goo•dohm*
denim	**jeans** *jeanz*
lace	**renda** *rehn•duh*
leather	**couro** *kau•roo*
linen	**linho** *lee•nyoo*
silk	**seda** *seh•thuh*
wool	**lã** *luh*
Is it machine washable?	**Isto é para lavar na máquina?** *ee•stoo eh puh•ruh luh•vahr nuh mah•kee•nuh*

Shoes

I'd like a pair of...	**Queria um par de...** *keh•ree•uh oong pahr deh...*
high-heeled/ flat shoes	**sapatos altos/baixos** *suh•pah•tooz ahl•tooz/ beye•shooz*
boots	**botas** *baw•tuhz*
loafers	**loafers** *loa•ferz*
sandals	**sandálias** *suhn•dah•lee•uhz*
shoes	**sapatos** *suh•pah•tooz*
slippers	**chinelas** *shee•neh•luhz*
sneakers	**tênis** *tehn•ehz*
In size...	**No tamanho...** *noo tuh•muh•nyoo...*

For Numbers, see page 173.

Sizes

small (S)	**pequeno** *peh•keh•noo*
medium (M)	**médio** *meh•dee•oo*
large (L)	**grande** *gruhnd*
extra large (XL)	**extra grande** *ay•struh gruhnd*
petite	**pequeno** *peh•keh•noo*
plus size	**tamanho de factor positivo** *tuh•muh•nyoo deh fah•taur poo•see•tee•voo*

Newsagent & Tobacconist

Do you sell English-language newspapers?	**Vende jornais em inglês?** *vehn•deh zsoor•neyez eng eeng•lehz*
I'd like...	**Queria...** *keh•ree•uh...*
candy [sweets]	**balas** *bah•luhz*
chewing gum	**goma de mascar** *gau•muh deh muhz•kahr*
a chocolate bar	**uma barra de chocolate** *oonga bar•rah deh shoo•koo•lah•teh*
a cigar	**um charuto** *oong shuh•roo•too*
I'd like...	**Queria...** *keh•ree•uh...*
a pack/carton of cigarettes	**um maço/pacote de cigarros** *oong mah•soo/puh•kaut deh see•gah•rrooz*
a lighter	**um isqueiro** *oong ees•kay•roo*
a magazine	**uma revista** *oo•muh reh•vee•stuh*
matches	**fósforos** *fawz•fuh•rooz*
a newspaper	**um jornal** *oong zsoorr•nahl*
a pen	**uma caneta** *oo•muh kuh•neh•tuh*
a postcard	**um postal** *oong poo•stahl*
a road/town map of...	**um mapa de/da cidade de...** *oong mah•puh deh/deh see•dahd deh...*
stamps	**selos** *seh•looz*

Photography

I'm looking for...camera.	**Estou à procura de [procurando] uma máquina fotográfica...** *ee•stawoo ah praw•koo•ruh deh [praw•koo•ruhn•doo] oo•muh mah•kee•nuh faw•too•grah•fee•kuh...*
an automatic	**automática** *ahoo•too•mah•tee•kuh*
a digital	**digital** *deh•zseh•tahl*
a disposable	**descartável** *dehz•kuhr•tah•vehl*
I'd like...	**Queria...** *keh•ree•uh...*
a battery	**uma pilha** *oo•muh pee•lyuh*
digital prints	**impressões digitais** *eem•preh•soingz deh•zseh•teyez*
a memory card	**um cartão de memória** *oong kuhr•tohm deh meh•maw•ree•uh*
Can I print digital photos here?	**Posso imprimir fotos digitais aqui?** *paw•soo eem•pree•meer faw•tooz deh•zeh•teyez uh•kee*

Souvenirs

bottle of wine	**a garrafa de vinho** *uh guh•rrah•fuh deh vee•nyoo*
box of chocolates	**a caixa de chocolates** *uh keye•shuh deh shoo•koo•lah•tehz*
calendar	**o calendário** *oo kuh•lehn•dah•ree•oo*
postcards	**postais** *pooz•teyez*
scarf	**o lenço** *oo lehn•soo*
souvenir guide	**o guia turístico** *oo gee•uh too•ree•stee•koo*
T-shirt	**a camiseta** *uh kuh•mee•seh•tuh*
toy/game	**o brinquedo/jogo** *oo breeng•keh•thoo/zsaw•goo*
wine	**o vinho** *oo vee•nyoo*
Can I see this/that?	**Posso ver este/esse?** *paw•soo vehr ehst/eh•seh*
It's the one in the window/display case.	**É aquele na janela/vitrine.** *eh uh•kehl nuh zsuh•neh•luh/vee•treen*

I'd like…	**Queria…** *keh•ree•uh…*
a battery	**uma pilha** *oo•muh pee•lyuh*
a bracelet	**uma pulseira** *oo•muh pool•say•ruh*
a brooch	**um broche** *oong brawsh*
earrings	**brincos** *breeng•kooz*
a necklace	**um colar** *oong koo•lahr*
a ring	**um anel** *oong uh•nehl*
a watch	**um relógio de pulso** *oong reh•loy•zsoo deh pool•soo*
copper	**cobre** *kaw•breh*
crystal	**cristal** *kree•stahl*
diamonds	**brilhantes** *bree•lyuhntz*
white/yellow gold	**ouro branco/amarelo** *au•roo bruhn•koo/ uh•muh•reh•loo*
pearls	**pérolas** *peh•roo•luhz*
pewter	**peltre** *pehl•treh*
platinum	**platina** *plah•tee•nuh*
sterling silver	**prata** *prah•tuh*
Is this real?	**É verdadeiro?** *eh vehr•duh•day•roo*
Can you engrave it?	**Pode gravá-lo?** *pawd gruh•vah•loo*

Ceramics such as clay bowls and water jugs are a particulary good purchase in the northeast, as well as clay figurines depicting folk heroes, customs and celebrations, and handmade lace and embroidered clothing. From the Amazon, look for Marajoara ceramic pieces decorated with geometric patterns. Straw and natural fibre baskets, hats, bags mats, etc. are all popular souvenirs too.
Afro-Brazilian musical instruments provide alternative ideas as presents. Some examples are **berimbau** (a stretched metal strip, played with a stick), **bongô** (bongo drums) and **atabaque** (another type of drum).

Sport & Leisure

ESSENTIAL

When's the game? **Quando é o jogo?** *kwuhn•doo eh o zsau•goo*
Where's...? **Onde é...?** *aund eh...*
the beach **a praia** *uh preye•uh*
the park **o parque** *oo pahr•keh*
the pool **a piscina** *uh pee•see•nuh*
Is it safe to swim here? **Pode nadar aqui sem perigo?** *pawd nuh•dahr uh•kee sehn peh•ree•goo*
Can I hire golf clubs? **Posso alugar tacos?** *paw•soo uh•loo•gahr tah•kooz*
How much per hour? **Qual é a tarifa por hora?** *kwahl eh uh tuh•ree•fuh poor aw•ruh*
How far is it to...? **A que distância fica...?** *uh keh dee•stuhn•see•uh fee•kuh...*
Can you show me on the map? **Pode indicar no mapa?** *pawd een•dee•kahr noo mah•puh*

Watching Sport

When's...? **Quando é...?** *kwuhn•doo eh...*
the basketball game **o jogo de basquetebol** *oo zsau•goo deh bah•skeht•bawl*
the boxing match **a partida de boxe** *uh puhr•tee•duh deh bawkz*
the cycling race **a corrida de bicicleta** *uh koo•ree•thuh deh bee•see•kleht*
the golf tournament **o torneio de golfe** *oo taur•nay•oo deh gawlf*
the soccer [football] game **o jogo de futebol** *oo zsau•goo deh foo•teh•bawl*

Brazilians are avid soccer fans and the sport unites all ages and classes. Rio boasts Maracanã, the largest soccer stadium in the world. Be warned, during World Cup season, the country grinds to a halt!

When's...? **Quando é...?** *kwuhn•doo eh...*
  the basketball game **o jogo de basquete** *oo zsau•goo deh bah•skeht*
  the tennis match **a partida de tênis** *uh puhr•tee•thuh de teh•neez*
  the volleyball game **o jogo de vôlei** *oo zsau•goo deh vaw•lay*
Which teams are playing? **Quais são os times que jogam?** *kweyez sohm ooz tee•mehs keh zsau•gohm*
Where's...? **Onde é...?** *aund eh...*
  the horsetrack **a pista de cavalo** *uh peez•tuh deh kuh•vah•loo*
  the racetrack **o hipódromo** *oo ee•paw•drau•moo*
  the stadium **o estádio** *oo uhs•tah•dee•oo*
Where can I place a bet? **Onde posso fazer uma aposta?** *aund paw•soo fah•zaer uh•paws•tuh*

Playing Sport

Where's...? **Onde é...?** *aund eh...*
  the golf course **o campo de golfe** *oo kuhm•poo deh gawlf*

the gym	**o clube desportivo [esportivo]** *oo kloob dehs•poor•tee•voo [ees•poor•tee•voo]*
the park	**o parque** *oo pahrk*
the tennis courts	**os campos [as quadras] de tênis** *ooz kuhm•pooz [uhz kwah•druhz] deh teh•neez*
How much per...?	**Qual é o preço por...?** *kwahl eh oo preh•soo poor...*
day	**dia** *dee•uh*
hour	**hora** *aw•ruh*
game	**jogo** *zsau•goo*
round	**volta** *vawl•tuh*
Can I rent [hire]...?	**Posso alugar...?** *paw•soo uh•loo•gahr...*
golf clubs	**tacos de golfe** *tah•kooz deh gawlf*
equipment	**o equipamento** *oo ee•kee•puh•mehn•too*
a racket	**uma raquete** *oo•muh rah•keht*

At the Beach/Pool

Where's the beach/pool?	**Onde é a praia/piscina?** *aund eh uh preye•uh/pee•see•nuh*
Is there...?	**Há...?** *ah...*
a kiddie pool	**uma piscina para crianças** *oo•muh pee•see•nuh puh•ruh kree•uhn•suhs*
an indoor/outdoor pool	**uma piscina coberta/ao ar livre** *oo•muh pee•see•nuh koo•behr•tuh/ahoo ahr lee•vreh*
a lifeguard	**uma salva-vidas** *oo•muh sahl•vuh vee•duhz*
Is it safe...?	**É perigoso...?** *eh per•ree•gau•zoo...*
to swim	**para nadar** *puh•ruh nuh•dahr*
to dive	**para mergulhar** *puh•ruh mehr•goo•lyahr*
for children	**para as crianças** *puh•ruh uhz kree•uhn•suhs*
I want to hire...	**Quero alugar...** *keh•roo uh•loo•gahr...*
a deck chair	**uma cadeira de encosto** *oo•muh kuh•day•ruh deh ehn•kaus•stoo*

diving equipment	**equipamento para mergulhar** *ee•kee•puh•mehn•too puh•ruh mehr•goo•lyahr*
a jet-ski	**um jet-ski** *oong zseht•skee*
a motorboat	**um barco a motor** *oong bahr•koo uh moo•taur*
a rowboat	**um barco a remos** *oong bahr•koo uh reh•mooz*
snorkling equipment	**equipamento de snorkling** *ee•kee•puh•mehn•too de snawr•kleeng*
a surfboard	**uma prancha de surf** *oo•muh pruhn•shuh deh soorf*
a towel	**uma toalha** *oo•muh too•ah•lyuh*
an umbrella	**um guarda sol** *oong gwahr•duh sawl*
water skis	**esquis-aquáticos** *eez•keez uh•kwah•tee•kooz*
a windsurfer	**uma prancha à vela** *oo•muh pruhn•shuh ah veh•luh*
For...hours.	**Por...horas.** *poor... aw•ruhz*

Brazil is practically synonymous with long stretches of golden beaches; **Copacabana** and **Ipanema** in Rio are known the world over. Surfing is popular all along the Brazilian coast, and beach volleyball is also a popular pursuit. The largest beaches have lifeguards, but look for the following swimming flags: red (swimming forbidden), yellow (swim near the beach), green (safe).

Brazil and its beaches are equally synonymous with tiny bikinis. The local **tanga** (string bikini) or **fio dental** (literally "dental floss") can be purchased everywhere, and many stores are solely dedicated to swimwear. Despite this however, don't forget that Brazil is a deeply Catholic and often conservative country. Topless sunbathing is regarded as offensive.

Out in the Country

I'd like a map...	**Queria um mapa...** *keh•ree•uh oong mah•puh...*
of this region	**desta região** *deh•stuh reh•zsee•ohm*
of the walking routes	**de roteiros a pé** *deh roh•tay•rooz a peh*
of bike routes	**de roteiros de bicicleta** *deh roh•tay•rooz deh bee•see•kleh•tuh*
of the trails	**dos caminhos** *thooz kuh•mee•nyooz*
Is it easy/difficult ?	**É fácil/difícil?** *eh fah•seel/dee•fee•seel*
Is it far/steep?	**É distante/íngreme?** *eh deez•tuhnt/een•grae•meh*
How far is it to...?	**A que distância fica...** *uh keh dee•stuhn•see•uh fee•kuh...*
Can you show me on the map?	**Pode indicar no mapa?** *pawd een•dee•kahr noo mah•puh*
I'm lost.	**Estou perdido** *m* **/perdida** *f.* *ee•stawoo pehr•dee•doo/pehr•dee•duh*
Where's...?	**Onde é...?** *aund eh...*
the bridge	**a ponte** *uh paunt*
the cave	**a caverna** *uh kuh•vehr•nuh*
the cliff	**a falésia** *uh fuh•leh•see•uh*
the desert	**o deserto** *oo deh•zehr•too*
the farm	**a fazenda** *uh fuh•zehn•dah*

the field	**o campo** *oo kuhm•poo*
the forest	**a floresta** *uh flau•reh•stuh*
the hill	**a colina** *uh koo•lee•nuh*
the lake	**o lago** *oo lah•goo*
the mountain	**a montanha** *uh maun•tah•nyuh*
the nature preserve	**a reserva natural** *uh reh•zehr•vuh nuh•too•rahl*
the view point	**o mirante** *oo mee•ruhnt*
the park	**o parque** *oo pahrk*
the path	**o caminho para pedestres** *oo kuh•mee•nyoo puh•ruh peh•dehs•trehz*
the peak	**o pico** *oo pee•koo*
the picnic area	**a área de piqueniques** *a ahr•ee•uh deh pee•keh•nee•kehz*
the pond	**a lagoa** *uh luh•gaw•uh*
the river	**o rio** *oo rree•oo*
the sea	**o mar** *oo mahr*
the valley	**o vale** *oo vahl*

Where's...?	**Onde é...?** *aund eh...*
the vineyard	**o vinhedo** *uh vee•nyeh•doo*
the waterfall	**a cachoeira** *uh kuh•shway•ra*
I want to hire...	**Quero alugar...** *eh•roo uh•loo•gahr...*
boots	**botas** *baw•tuhz*
a helmet	**um capacete** *oong kuh•puh•seht*
These are too big/small.	**Estes são muito grandes/pequenos.** *ehs•tehz sohm mooee•too gruhn•dehz/pee•keh•nooz*
Are there lessons?	**Tem aulas?** *Teng ahoo•laz*
I'm a beginner.	**Sou principiante.** *sawoo preen•see•puhnt*
I'm experienced.	**Tenho experiência.** *teh•nyoo ees•peh•ree•ehn•see•uh*
A trail [piste] map, please.	**Um mapa da trilha, por favor.** *oong mah•puh deh tree•lyuh poor fuh•vaur*

YOU MAY SEE...

BONDE/FUNICULAR	cable car/gondola
TELEFÉRICO	chair lift
INICIANTE	novice
INTERMEDIÁRIO	intermediate
AVANÇADO	expert
PISTA FECHADA	trail [piste] closed

Going Out

ESSENTIAL

What is there to do in the evenings?	**O que há para se fazer à noite?** *oo keh ah puh•ruh seh fuh•zehr ah noyt*
Do you have a program of events?	**Tem um programa dos espectáculos?** *teng oong proo•gruh•muh dooz ee•spehk•tah•koo•looz*
What's playing at the movies [cinema] tonight?	**O que está passando no cinema hoje à noite?** *oo kee ee•stah pah•san•doh noo see•neh•muh auzseh ah noyt*
Where's...?	**Onde é...?** *aund eh...*
the downtown area	**o centro** *oo sehn•troo*
the bar	**o bar** *oo bar*
the dance club	**a discoteca** *uh deez•koo•teh•kuh*
Is there a cover charge?	**É preciso pagar entrada [ingresso]?** *eh preh•see•zoo puh•gahr ehn•trah•duh [een•greh•soo]*

Entertainment

Can you recommend...?	**Pode recomendar...?** *pawd reh•koo•mehn•dahr...*
a concert	**um concerto** *oong kaun•sehr•too*
a movie	**um filme** *oong feel•meh*
an opera	**uma ópera** *oo•muh aw•peh•ruh*
a play	**uma peça de teatro** *oo•muh peh•ssah duh tee•ah•troo*
When does it start/end?	**A que horas começa/acaba?** *uh kee aw•ruhz koo•meh•suh/uh•kah•buh*
What's the dress code?	**Qual é o traje apropriado?** *Kwal eh oo trahj ah•praw•pree•ah•doo*

I like...	**Gosto de...** *gaws•too deh...*
classical music	**música clássica** *moo•zee•kuh klah•see•kuh*
folk music	**música popular** *moo•zee•kuh poo•poo•lahr*
jazz	**jazz** *zsahz*
pop music	**pop** *pawp*
rap	**rap** *rahp*

For Tickets, see page 20.

Carnaval is widely celebrated in Brazil. A time of lavish celebration before Lent, **Carnaval** begins four days before Ash Wednesday, and ends with the famous 'Fat Tuesday' celebration. Look for parades on the streets and carnival balls (**bailes carnavalescos**). The famed **Carnaval do Rio** sees the spectacularly colorful competition between the various samba schools in a parade through the streets of Rio de Janeiro.

Samba and **bossa nova** are the dance styles best known abroad, but look out for regional rhythms like **pagode**, **lambada**, **frevo**, **forró**, **maracatu**, **baião**, **carimbó** and **bumba-meu boi**, with their mixture of African, Indian, and European influences.

Local papers and weekly entertainment guides such as **Veja** will tell you what's on and have good restaurant listings too. Regional booklets (**vejinha**) are also useful. To purchase tickets online in advance, try www.ingresso.com.br. It is good for movies, shows and theme parks. For sporting events, try www.ingressofacil.com.br. Alternatively, Ticketmaster also sells tickets for shows, concerts and sporting events.

Nightlife

What is there to do in the evenings?	**O que há para se fazer à noite?** *oo keh ah puh•ruh seh fuh•zehr ah noyt*
Can you recommend…?	**Pode recomendar…?** *pawd reh•koo•mehn•dahr…*
a bar	**um bar** *oong bar*
a casino	**um casino** *oong kuh•see•noo*
a dance club	**uma discoteca** *oo•muh dee•skoo•teh•kuh*
a gay club	**um clube gay** *oong kloob gay*
a jazz club	**um clube de jazz** *oong kloob deh zsahz*
a club with Brazilian music?	**uma discoteca com música brasileira?** *oo•muh dee•skoo•teh•kuh kaum moo•zee•kuh bruh•see•lay•ruh*
Is there live music?	**Há música ao vivo?** *ah moo•zee•kuh ahoo vee•voo*
How do I get there?	**Como é que vou até lá?** *kau•moo eh keh vauoo uh•teh lah*
Is there a cover charge?	**É preciso pagar entrada [ingresso]?** *eh preh•see•zoo puh•gahr ehn•trah•duh [een•greh•soo]*

Let's go dancing. **Vamos dançar.** *vuh•mooz duhn•sahr*

Is this area safe at night? **Esta área é segura à noite?** *eh•stuh ah•rryah eh seh•goo•ruh ah noyt?*

YOU MAY HEAR...

Desligue os seus celulares, por favor. *dehz•lee•geh oohz sehooz sehl•oo•lahrz poor fuh•vaur* Turn off your cell [mobile] phones, please.

Special Requirements

Business Travel

ESSENTIAL

I'm here on business.	**Estou aqui a negócios.** *ee•stawoo uh•kee ah neh•gaw•see•oosz*
Here's my business card.	**Tome o meu cartão.** *taw•meh oo meeoo kuhr•tohm*
Can I have your card?	**Por favor, o seu cartão?** *poor fuh•vaur oo sehoo kuhr•tohm*
I have a meeting with...?	**Tenho uma reunião com...** *tay•nyoo oomah rree•oo•nee•ohm kaum...*
Where's...?	**Onde é...** *aund eh...*
the business center	**o centro de negócios** *oo sehn•troo deh neh•gaw•see•oosz*
the convention hall	**a sala de convenção** *ah sah•lah deh kaun•vehn•sohmz*
the meeting room	**a sala de reunião** *ah sah•lah deh rree•oo•nee•ohmz*

On Business

I'm here to attend...	**Estou aqui para participar...** *ee•stawoo uh•kee puh•ruh puhr•tee•see•pahr...*
a seminar	**de um seminário** *deh oong seh•mee•nah•ree•oo*
a conference	**de uma conferência** *deh oomuh kaun•feh•rehn•see•uh*
a meeting	**de uma reunião** *deh oomuh rree•oo•nee•ohm*
My name is...	**Meu nome é...** *mehoo naum•ee eh...*
May I introduce my colleague...	**Posso apresentar o meu colega** *m* **/a minha colega** *f*... *paw•soo uh•preh•zehn•tahr oo mehoo koo•leh•guh/uh mee•nyuh koo•leh•guh...*

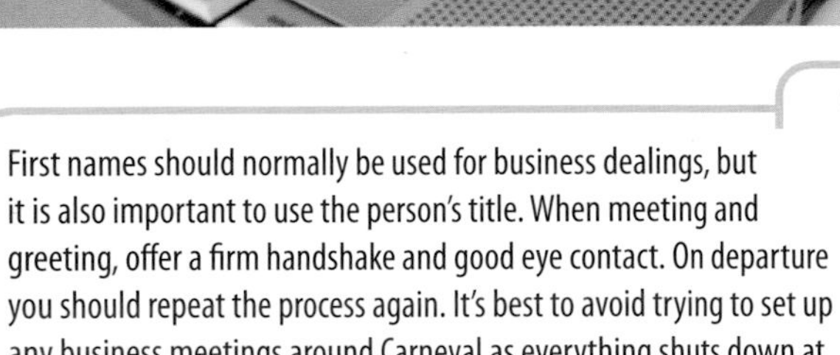

First names should normally be used for business dealings, but it is also important to use the person's title. When meeting and greeting, offer a firm handshake and good eye contact. On departure you should repeat the process again. It's best to avoid trying to set up any business meetings around Carneval as everything shuts down at this time.

I have a meeting/ an appointment with...	**Tenho uma reunião com...** *tay•nyoo oo•muh rree•oo•nee•ohm kaum...*
I'm sorry I'm late.	**Desculpe, estou atrasado** *m* **/atrasada** *f.* *dehs•kool•puh ee•stawoo uh•truh•zah•thoo/ uh•truh•zah•thuh*
I need an interpreter.	**Preciso de um tradutor.** *preh•see•zoo deh oong truh•doo•taur*
You can reach me at the...Hotel.	**Pode me encontrar no hotel...** *pawd•eh meh eng•kaun•trahr noo aw•tehl...*
I'm here until...	**Estou aqui até...** *ee•stawoo uh•kee uh•teh...*

I need to... **Preciso de...** *preh•see•zoo deh...*

make a call **fazer um telefonema** *fuh•zehr oong teh•leh•faw•neh•muh*

make a photocopy **fazer uma fotocópia** *fuh•zehr oo•muh faw•taw•kaw•pee•uh*

send an e-mail **enviar um e-mail** *eng•vee•ahr oong ee•mehl*

send a fax **enviar um fax** *ehn•vee•ahr oong fahks*

send a package (overnight) **enviar um embrulho (de um dia para o outro)** *ehn•vee•ahr oong eng•broo•lyoo (deh oong dee•uh puh•ruh oo aw•troo)*

It was a pleasure to meet you. **Muito prazer.** *mooee•too pruh•zehr*

For Communications, see page 52.

YOU MAY HEAR...

Você tem uma hora marcado? *vaw•seh teng oo•muh oh•rah mahr•cah•doo* Do you have an appointment?

Com quem? *kaum keng* With whom?

Está numa reunião. *ee•stah noo•muh ree•oo•nee•ohm* He/She is in a meeting.

Um momento, por favor. *oong moo•mehn•too poor fuh•vaur* One moment, please.

Sente-se. *sehn•tuh•suh* Have a seat.

Quer alguma coisa para beber? *kehr ahl•goo•mah coy•zuh puh•ruh beh•behr* Would you like something to drink?

Obrigado *m* **/Obrigada** *f* **por vir.** *aw•bree•gah•thoo/aw•bree•gah•thuh poor veer* Thank you for coming.

Traveling with Children

ESSENTIAL

Is there a discount for children?	**Há desconto para crianças?** *ah dehs•caun•too puh•ruh kree•uhn•suhs*
Can you recommend a babysitter?	**Pode recomendar-me uma babysitter [babá] qualificada?** *pawd reh•koo•mehn•dahr•meh oo•muh bay•bee•sit•tur [bah•buh] kwahl•ee•fee•kah•duh*
Do you have a child's seat/ highchair?	**Pode trazer uma cadeirinha de criança/ cadeira alta?** *pawd truh•zehr oo•muh kuh•day•ree•nyuh deh kree•uhn•suh/ kuh•day•ruh ahl•tuh*
Where can I change the baby?	**Onde posso trocar o bebê [neném]?** *aund paw•soo traw•kahr oo beh•beh [neh•neh]*

Out & About

Can you recommend something for the kids?	**Pode recomendar algo próprio para crianças?** *pawd reh•koo•mehn•dahr ahl•goo praw•pree•oo puh•ruh kree•uhn•suhs*
Where's…?	**Onde é…?** *aund eh…*
the amusement park	**o parque de diversões** *oo pahr•keh deh dee•vehr•sohmz*
the arcade	**o salão de jogos** *oo suh•lohm deh zsaw•gooz*
the kiddie [paddling] pool	**a piscina de bebês [nenéns]** *uh pee•see•nuh deh beh•behz [neh•nehnz]*
the park	**o parque** *oo pahrk*
the playground	**o playground** *oo play•graund*
the zoo	**o jardim zoológico** *oo zsuhr•deem zoo•law•zsee•koo*
Are kids allowed?	**São permitidas crianças?** *sohm pehr•mee•tee•thuhz kree•uhn•suhz*

Is it safe for kids?	**É seguro para as crianças?** *eh seh•goo•roo puh•ruh uhz kree•uhn•suhs*
Is it suitable for... year olds?	**Será bom para crianças com...anos?** *seh•rah bohng puh•ruh kree•uhn•suhz kaum... uh•nooz*

YOU MAY HEAR...

Que gracinha/bonitinho! *keh grah•see•nyah/boo•nee•tee•nyo*	How cute!
Qual o nome dele/dela? *kwal oo nau•meh dehl/deh•luh*	What's his/her name?
Quantos anos ele/ela tem? *kwuh•tooz uh•nooz ehl/eh•luh teng*	How old is he/she?

Baby Essentials

Do you have...?	**Tem...?** *teng...*
a baby bottle	**uma mamadeira** *oo•muh muh•muh•deh•rah*
baby wipes	**os lenços umedecidos para o bebê [nenê]** *ooz lehn•sawz oo•muh•duh•see•duhz puh•ruh oo beh•beh [neh•neh]*

a car seat	**um assento de carro** *oong uh•sehn•too deh kah•rroo*
a children's menu/ portion	**uma porção de criança** *oo•muh poor•sohm deh kree•uhn•suh*
a child's seat	**uma cadeirinha de criança** *oo•muh kuh•day•ree•nyuh deh kree•uhn•suh*
a crib	**uma cama de bebê [neném]** *oo•muh kuh•muh deh beh•beh [neh•neh]*
diapers [nappies]	**as fraldas** *uhz frahl•duhz*
formula	**fórmula de bebê [neném]** *fawr•moo•luh deh beh•beh [neh•neh]*
a pacifier [dummy]	**uma chupeta** *oo•muh shoo•peh•tuh*
a playpen	**um parque para crianças** *oong pahr•kuh puh•ruh kree•uhn•suhz*
a stroller [pushchair]	**uma cadeira de bebê [neném]** *oo•muh kuh•day•ruh deh beh•beh [neh•neh]*
Can I breastfeed the baby here?	**Posso amamentar o bebê [neném] aqui?** *paw•soo uh•muh•mehn•tahr oo beh•beh [neh•neh] uh•kee*
Where can I change the baby?	**Onde posso trocar o bebê [neném]?** *aund paw•soo traw•kahr oo beh•beh [neh•neh]*

For Dining with Children, see page 68.

Babysitting

Can you recommend a reliable babsitter?	**Pode recomendar uma babysitter [babá] qualificada?** *pawd reh•koo•mehn•dahr oo•muh bay•bee•sit•tur [bah•bah] kwah•lee•fee•kah•thuh*
What's the charge?	**Qual é o preço?** *kwahl eh oo preh•soo*
I'll be back by…	**Volto às…** *vawl•too ahz…*
I can be reached at…	**Pode me encontrar…** *pawd meh ng•kaun•trahr…*

For Time, see page 175.

Health & Emergency

Can you recommend a pediatrician?	**Pode recomendar um pediatra?** *pawd reh•kau•mehn•dahr oong pee•dee•ah•truh*
My child is allergic to…	**A minha criança é alérgico** *m* **/alérgica** *f* **a…** *uh mee•nyuh kree•uhn•suh eh uh•lehr•gee•koo/ uh•lehr•gee•kuh uh…*
My son/daughter is missing.	**O meu filho/A minha filha desapareceu.** *oo mehoo fee•lyoo/uh mee•nyuh fee•lyuh deh•zuh•puh•ruh•seoo*
Have you seen a boy/ girl?	**Viu um menino/uma menina?** *veeoo oong meh•nee•noo/oo•muh meh•nee•nuh*

For Health, see page 159.

Disabled Travelers

ESSENTIAL

Is there…?	**Há…?** *ah…*
access for the disabled	**acesso para deficientes físicos** *uh•seh•soo puh•ruh deh•fee•see•ehntz fee•see•kooz*
a wheelchair ramp	**uma rampa de cadeira de rodas** *oo•muh ruhm•puh deh kuh•day•ruh deh raw•thuhz*
a handicapped- [disabled-] accessible toilet	**um banheiro acessível para deficientes** *oong buh•nyay•rooz uh•seh•see•vehl puh•ruh deh•fee•see•ehntz*
I need…	**Preciso de…** *preh•see•zoo deh…*
assistance	**assistência** *uh•see•stehn•see•uh*
an elevator [lift]	**um elevador** *oong eh•leh•vuh•daur*
a ground-floor room	**um quarto no primeiro andar** *oong kwahr•too noo pree•may•roo uhn•dahr*

Asking for Assistance

I'm disabled.	**Sou deficiente.** *sawoo deh•fee•see•ehnt*
I'm deaf.	**Sou surdo** *m* **/Sou surda** *f*. *sawoo soor•doo/sawoo soor•duh*
I'm visually/hearing impaired.	**Vejo/Ouço mal.** *vay•zsoo/ow•soo mahl*
I'm unable to walk far/ use the stairs.	**Não posso caminhar muito/usar as escadas.** *nohm paw•soo kuh•mee•nyahr mween•tuh/oo•zahr uhz ee•skah•thuhz*
Please speak louder.	**Por favor, fale mais alto.** *poor fuh•vaur fah•leh mey•ez ahl•too*
Can I bring my wheelchair?	**Posso trazer a minha cadeira de rodas?** *paw•soo truh•zehr uh mee•nyuh kuh•day•ruh deh raw•duhz*
Are guide dogs permitted?	**Os cães de guia são permitidos?** *ooz kengs de gee•uh sohm pehr•mee•tee•dooz*
Can you help me?	**Pode me ajudar?** *pawd meh uh•zsoo•dahr*
Please open/hold the door.	**Por favor abra/segure a porta.** *poor fuh•vaur ah•bruh/seh•goo•reh uh pawr•tuh*

In an Emergency

Emergencies

ESSENTIAL

Help!	**Socorro!** *soo•kau•rroo*
Go away!	**Vá embora!** *vah ehng•baw•ruh*
Call the police!	**Chame a polícia!** *shuh•meh uh poo•lee•see•uh*
Stop thief!	**Pare o ladrão!** *pah•ree oo luh•drohm*
Get a doctor!	**Chame um médico!** *shuh•meh oong meh•dee•koo*
Fire!	**Fogo!** *fau•goo*
I'm lost.	**Estou perdido** *m* **/perdida** *f***.** *ee•stawoo pehr•dee•thoo/pehr•dee•thuh*
Can you help me?	**Pode me ajudar?** *pawd meh uh•zsoo•dahr*

In an emergency, dial **190** for the police, **192** for the ambulance, and **193** for the fire brigade.

YOU MAY HEAR...

Preencha este formulário. *pree•eng•sheh eh•stuh fawr•muh•lah•reeoo*	Fill out this form.
A sua identificação, por favor. *uh soo•uh ee•dehnt•tee•fee•kuh•sohm por fuh•vaur*	Your identification, please.
Quando/Onde é que foi? *kwuhn•doo/aund eh keh foy*	When/Where did it happen?
Como é ele/ela? *kau•moo eh ehleh/ehluh*	What does he/she look like?

Police

ESSENTIAL

Call the police!	**Chame a polícia!** *shuh•meh uh poo•lee•see•uh*
Where's the police station?	**Onde é a delegacia de polícia?** *aund eh uh deh•leh•guh•see•uh thuh poo•lee•see•uh*
There has been an accident/attack.	**Houve um acidente/ataque.** *auoo•veh oong uh•see•dehnt/uh•tah•keh*
My son/daughter is missing.	**O meu filho/A minha filha desapareceu.** *oo mehoo fee•lyoo/uh mee•nyuh fee•lyuh deh•zuh•puh•ruh•seoo*
I need…	**Preciso de…** *preh•see•zoo deh…*
an interpreter	**um tradutor** *oong truh•doo•taur*
I need…	**Preciso de…** *preh•see•zoo deh…*
to contact my lawyer	**contatar o meu advogado** *kaun•tuh•tahr oo mehoo uhd•voo•gah•thoo*
to make a phone call	**fazer um telefonema** *fuh•zehr oong teh•leh•foo•neh•muh*
I'm innocent.	**Sou inocente.** *sawoo ee•naw•sehnt*

Crime & Lost Property

I want to report…	**Quero reportar…** *keh•roo reh•paur•tahr…*
a mugging	**um assalto** *oong uh•sahl•too*
a rape	**um estupro** *oong ee•stoo•proo*
a theft	**um roubo** *oong rau•boo*
I've been robbed.	**Fui roubado *m* /roubada *f*.** *fooee raw•bah•thoo/ raw•bah•thuh*

I've been mugged.	**Fui assaltado** *m* **/assaltada** *f.* *fooee uh•sahl•tah•thoo/uh•sahl•tah•duh*
I've lost my...	**Perdi...** *pehr•thee...*
My...has/have been stolen.	**Roubaram a minha/o meu...** *raw•bah•rohm ah minya/ oo maehoo...*
backpack	**a mochila** *uh moo•sheeh•luh*
bicycle	**a bicicleta** *uh bee•see•kleh•tuh*
camera	**a máquina fotográfica** *uh mah•kee•nuh faw•too•grah•fee•kuh*
(hire) car	**o carro (alugado)** *oo kah•rroo (uh•loo•gah•doo)*
computer	**o computador** *oo kaum•poo•tuh•daur*
credit card	**os cartão de crédito** *ooz kuhr•tohm deh kreh•dee•too*
jewelry	**as jóias** *uhz zsoy•uhz*
money	**o dinheiro** *oo dee•nyay•roo*
passport	**o passaporte** *oo pah•suh•pawrt*
purse [handbag]	**a carteira** *uh kuhr•tay•truh*
traveler's checks [cheques]	**os cheques de viagem.** *ooz shehkz deh vee•ah•zseng*
wallet	**a carteira (de documentos)** *uh kuhr•tay•ruh (deh doo•koo•mehn•tooz)*

I need a police report.	**Preciso de um documento da policia.** *preh•see•zoo deh oong thoo•koo•mehn•too duh poo•lee•see•uh*
Where is the British/American/Irish embassy?	**Onde fica a embaixada Britânica/Americana/Irlandesa?** *aund fee•kuh uh ehm•beye•shah•duh bree•tuhn•nee•kuh/uh•meh•ree•kuh•nuh/eer•luhn•deh•zuh*

Health

ESSENTIAL

I'm sick [ill].	**Estou doente.** *ee•stawoo doo•ehnt*
I need an English-speaking doctor.	**Preciso de um médico que fale inglês.** *preh•see•zoo deh oong meh•dee•koo keh fah•leh eeng•lehz*
It hurts here.	**Dói aqui.** *doy uh•kee*
I have a stomachache.	**Tenho dor de estômago.** *teh•nyoo daur deh ee•stau•muh•goo*

Finding a Doctor

Can you recommend a doctor/dentist?	**Pode recomendar um médico/dentista?** *pawd reh•koo•mehn•dahr oong meh•dee•koo dehn•teeh•stuh*
Could the doctor come to see me here?	**O médico podia vir aqui me ver?** *oo meh•dee•koo poo•thee•uh veer uh•kee meh vehr*
I need an English-speaking doctor.	**Preciso de um médico que fale inglês.** *preh•see•zoo deh oong meh•dee•koo keh fah•leh eeng•lehz*

What are the office hours?	**A que horas é a consulta?** *uh kee aw•ruhz eh ah kaun•sool•tuh*
I'd like to make an appointment…	**Queria marcar uma consulta…** *keh•ree•uh muhr•kahr oo•muh kaun•sool•tuh…*
for today	**para hoje** *puh•ruh auyzseh*
for tomorrow	**para amanhã** *puh•ruh uh•muh•nyuh*
as soon as possible	**o mais cedo possível** *oo meyez seh•thoo poo•see•vel*
It's urgent.	**É urgente.** *eh oor•zsehnt*

Symptoms

I'm…	**Estou…** *ee•stawoo…*
bleeding	**sangrando** *suhn•gruhn•doo*
constipated	**resfriado *m* /resfriada *f*** *rehz•free•ah•do /oong rehz•free•ah•da*
dizzy	**com tontura** *kaum tohn•too•rra*
I'm nauseous.	**Estou enjoado *m* /enjoada *f*.** *ee•stawoo eng•zsoo•ah•thoo/eng•zsoo•ah•thuh*
I'm vomiting.	**Estou vomitando.** *ee•stawoo voo•mee•tahn.do*
It hurts here.	**Dói aqui.** *doy uh•kee*
I have…	**Tenho…** *teh•nyoo…*
an allergic reaction	**uma reação alérgica** *oo•muh rree•ah•sohm uh•lehr•gee•kuh*
chest pain	**dor no peito** *daur noo pay•too*
diarrhea	**diarreia** *dee•uh•rray•uh*
an earache	**dor de ouvidos** *daur deh aw•vee•thooz*
a fever	**uma febre** *oo•muh feh•breh*
pain	**dor** *daur*
a rash	**uma erupção cutânea** *oo•muh eer•oop•sohm koo•tuh•nee•uh*

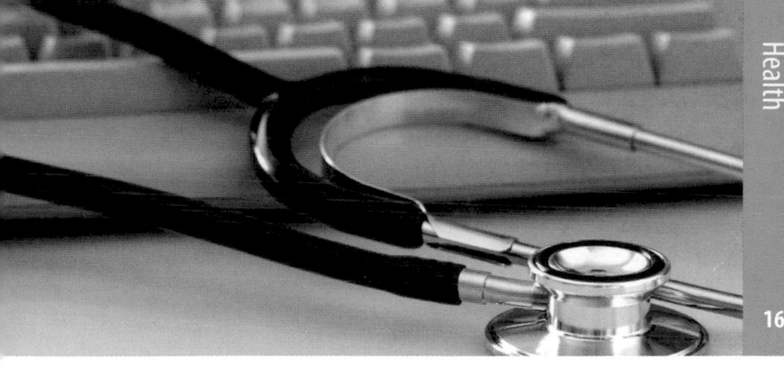

a sprain	**uma distensão muscular** *oo•muh dees•tehn•sohm moos•koo•lahr*
some swelling	**um inchaço** *oong een•shah•soo*
a stomachache	**dor de estômago** *daur deh ee•stau•muh•goo*
sunstroke.	**uma insolação.** *oo•muh een•soo•luh•sohm*
I've been sick [ill] for. . . days.	**Há. . .dias que me sinto doente.** *ah. . . dee•uhz keh meh seen•too doo•ehnt*

For Numbers, see page 173.

Conditions

I'm. . .	**Sou. . .** *sawoo. . .*
anemic	**anêmico** *m* **/anêmica** *f uh•neh•mee•koo/ uh•neh•mee•kuh*
asthmatic	**asmático** *m* **/asmática** *f uhz•mah•tee•koo/ uhz•mah•tee•kuh*
diabetic	**diabético** *m* **/diabética** *f dee•uh•beh•tee•koo/ dee•uh•beh•tee•kuh*
epileptic	**epilético** *eh•pee•leh•tee•koo*
I'm allergic to	**Sou alérgico** *m* **/alérgica** *f* **a**

antibiotics/penicillin.	**antibióticos penicilina.** *sawoo uh•lehr•gee•koo/ uh•lehr•gee•kuh uh uhn•tee•bee•aw•tee•kuhz/ peh•neh•seh•lee•nuh*
I have arthritis.	**Tenho artrite.** *teh•nyoo uh•treet*
I have a heart condition.	**Tenho um problema de coração.** *teh•nyoo oong proo•bleh•muh deh koo•ruh•sohm*
I have high/low blood pressure.	**Tenho a pressão arterial alta/baixa.** *teh•nyoo uh preh•sohm uhr•teh•ree•ahl ahl•tuh/beye•shuh*
I'm on…	**Estou tomando…** *ee•stawoo to•muhn•doo…*

YOU MAY HEAR…

Qual é o problema? *kwahl eh oo proo•bleh•muh*	What's the problem?
Onde é que dói? *aund eh keh doy*	Where does it hurt?
Dói aqui? *doy uh•kee*	Does it hurt here?
Toma medicamentos? *taw•muh meh•dee•kuh•mehn•tooz*	Are you on medication?
É alérgico *m* **/alérgica** *f* **a algo?** *eh uh•lehr•zsee•koo/uh•lehr•zsee•kuh uh ahl•goo*	Are you allergic to anything?
Abra a boca. *ah•bruh uh bau•kuh*	Open your mouth.
Respire fundo. *rehs•pee•reh foon•doo*	Breathe deeply.
Tussa, por favor. *too•suh, poor fuh•vaur*	Cough, please.
Quero que vá para o hospital. *keh•roo keh vah puh•ruh oo aws•pee•tahl*	I want you to go to the hospital.

Treatment

Do I need medicine?	**Preciso de algum medicamento?** *preh•see•zoo deh ahl•goong meh•dee•kuh•mehn•too*
Can you prescribe a generic drug [unbranded medication]?	**Pode prescrever um medicamento genérico** *pawd prehz•kreh•vehr oong meh•dee•kuh•mehn•too geh•neh•ree•koo*
Where can I get it?	**Onde posso obtê-lo?** *aund paw•soo au•bteh•loo*

For What to Take, see page 166.

Hospital

Please notify my family.	**Por favor informe a minha família.** *poor fuh•vaur eeng•fawr•meh uh mee•nyuh fuh•mee•lyuh*
I'm in pain.	**Estou com dores.** *ee•stawoo kaun daur•ehz*
I need a doctor/nurse.	**Necessito um médico/uma enfermeira.** *neh•seh•see•too oong meh•dee•koo/oo•muh een•fehr•may•ruh*
When are visiting hours?	**Quais são as horas de visitas?** *kweyez sohm uhz aw•ruhz deh vee•zee•tuhz*
I'm visiting…	**Estou visitando…** *ee•stawoo vee•see•tahn•doo…*

Dentist

I've broken a tooth/ lost a filling.	**Quebrei um dente./Minha restauração caiu.** *keh•bree oong dehnt/minia hes•tahoo•rrah•sohm kah•ee•oo*
I have a toothache.	**Tenho dor de dentes.** *teh•nyoo daur deh dehntz*
Can you fix this denture?	**Pode consertar esta dentadura?** *pawd kaun•sehr•tahr eh•stuh dehn•tuh•doo•ruh*

Gynecologist

I have menstrual cramps/a vaginal infection.	**Tenho dores menstruais/ uma infecção na vagina.** *teh•nyoo daurz mehn•stroo•eyez/oo•muh eeng•feh•sohm nuh vuh•zsee•nuh*
I missed my period.	**Não tive a última menstruação.** *Nohm teev ah ool•tee•mah mehn•strooas•ohn*
I'm on the pill.	**Estou tomando a pílula.** *ee•stawoo too•muhn•doo uh pee•loo•luh*
I'm (not) pregnant.	**(Não) Estou grávida.** *(nohm) ee•stawoo grah•vee•thuh*
I haven't had my period for...months.	**Já não menstruo há...meses.** *zsah nohm mehn•stroo•oh ah...meh•zehz*

Optician

I've lost...	**Perdi...** *pehr•thee...*
one of my contact lenses	**uma das minhas lentes de contato** *oo•muh duhz mee•nyuhz lehn•tehz deh kaun•tah•too*
my glasses	**os meus óculos** *ooz mehooz aw•koo•looz*
a lens	**uma lente** *oo•muh lehnt*

Payment & Insurance

How much?	**Quanto é?** *kwuhn•too eh*
Can I pay by credit card?	**Posso pagar com cartão de crédito?** *paw•soo puh•gahr kaum oo kuhr•tohm deh kreh•dee•too*
I have insurance.	**Tenho seguro.** *teh•nyoo seh•goo•roo*
Can you give me a receipt for my health insurance?	**Podia me dar um recibo para o meu seguro de saúde?** *poo•dee•uh meh dar oong reh•see•boo puh•ruh oo mehoo seh•goo•roo deh suh•oo•theh*

Pharmacy

ESSENTIAL

Where's the pharmacy [chemist]?	**Onde fica a farmácia?** *aund fee•kuh uh fuhr•mah•see•uh*
What time does the pharmacy open/close?	**A que horas abre/fecha a farmácia?** *uh keh aw•ruhz ah•breh/feh•shuh uh fuhr•mah•see•uh*
What would you recommend for...?	**O que é que me recomenda para...?** *oo keh eh keh meh reh•koo•mehn•duh puh•ruh...*
How much should I take?	**Quanto devo tomar?** *kwuhn•too deh•voo too•mahr*
Can you fill [make up] this prescription for me?	**Pode prescrever esta receita?** *pawd prehz•kreh•vehr eh•stuh reh•say•tuh*
I'm allergic to...	**Sou alérgico** *m* **/alérgica** *f* **a...** *sawoo uh•lehr•zsee•koo/uh•lehr•zsee•kuh ah...*

Pharmacies (**farmácia**) are easy to find and are often located at main intersections in busy areas. Drugs (**remédios**) are usually quite cheap too as they are subsidised by the government. Pharmacists in Brazil can also make a diagnosis if required and they can also administer vaccinations (**injeção**). For all-night pharmacies (**farmácia de serviço**), you should find the address of the one closest to you displayed in the window.

In the pharmacies in Brazil, you can normally find medicines, perfume, cosmetics and household goods. Travelers who use prescription medicine should bring enough with them to cover their stay.

What to Take

How much should I take?	**Quanto é que devo tomar?** *kwuhn•too eh keh deh•voo too•mahr*
How often should I take it?	**Quantas vezes devo tomar?** *kwuhn•tuhz veh•zehz deh•voo too•mahr*
Is it suitable for children?	**É próprio para crianças?** *eh praw•pree•oo puh•ruh kree•uhn•suhs*
I'm taking...	**Estou tomando...** *ee•stawoo uh too•mahn•doo...*

YOU MAY SEE...

UMA VEZ/TRÊS VEZES POR DIA	once/three times a day
COMPRIMIDO(S)	tablet(s)
GOTA	drop
COLHER(ES) DE CHÁ	teaspoon(s)
ANTES DAS/DEPOIS DAS/COM AS REFEIÇÕES	before/after/with meals
COM O ESTÔMAGO VAZIO	on an empty stomach
INGIRA INTEIRO	swallow whole
PODE CAUSAR SONOLÊNCIA	may cause drowsiness
PARA USO EXTERNO	for external use only

Are there side effects? **Há efeitos colaterais?** *ah ee•fay•tooz kaw•luh•tehr•eyez*

I'd like some medicine for... **Queria um remédio para...** *keh•ree•uh oohn ruh•meh•dee•oo puh•ruh...*

a cold **um resfriado** *oong rehz•free•ah•do*

a cough **a tosse** *uh taw•seh*

diarrhea **diarreia** *dee•uh•rray•uh*

a headache **dor de cabeça** *daur deh kuh•beh•suh*

insect bites **picadas de insecto** *pee•kah•duhz deh eeng•sehk•too*

motion sickness **enjoo** *ehn•zsau•oo*

a sore throat **dor de garganta** *daur deh guhr•guhn•tuh*

sunburn **queimadura de sol** *kay•muh•doo•ruh deh sawl*

a toothache **dor de dentes** *daur deh dehnts*

an upset stomach **uma dor de estômago** *oo•muh daur deh staw•muh•goo*

Basic Supplies

I'd like... **Queria...** *keh•ree•uh...*

acetaminophen [paracetamol] **paracetamol** *puh•ruh•seh•tuh•mawl*

antiseptic cream **pomada antiséptica** *poo•mah•duh uhn•tee•sehp•tee•kuh*

aspirin **aspirina** *uhz•pee•ree•nuh*

bandages **umas ataduras** *oo•muhz lee•guh•doo•ruhz uh•tuh•doo•ruhz*

a comb **um pente** *oong pehnt*

condoms **preservativos** *preh•sehr•vuh•tee•vooz*

contact lens solution **um líquido de lente de contato** *oong lee•kee•thoo deh lehnt deh kaun•tah•too*

deodorant **um desodorante** *oong dehz•aw•doo•ruhnt*

a hairbrush	**uma escova de cabelo** *oo•muh ees•kau•vuh deh kuh•beh•loo*
I'd like...	**Queria...** *keh•ree•uh...*
hair spray	**laquê para o cabelo** *lah•keh puh•ruh oo kuh•beh•loo*
ibuprofen	**ibuprofeno** *ee•boo•praw•feh•noo*
insect repellent	**repelente para insetos** *reh•peh•lehnt puh•ruh een•seh•tooz*
a nail file	**uma lixa** *oo•muh lee•shah*
a (disposable) razor	**gilete (descartável)** *zsee•leht (dush•kuhr•tah•vehl)*
razor blades	**lâminas de barbear** *luh•mee•nuhz deh buhr•bee•ahr*
sanitary napkins [towels]	**absorventes higiénicos** *uhb•sawr•vehntz ee•zseh•nee•kooz*
shampoo/ conditioner	**xampu/condicionador para cabelo** *shuhm•poo/ kaun•dee•see•oo•nuh•daur puh•ruh kuh•beh•lo*
soap	**sabonete** *suh•boo•neht*
sunscreen	**protetor solar** *praw•teh•taur soo•lahr*
tampons	**uns tampões higiênicos** *oongz tuhm•poingz ee•zseh•nee•kooz*
tissues	**lenços de papel** *lehn•sooz deh puh•pehl*
toilet paper	**papel higiênico** *puh•pehl ee•zseh•nee•koo*
toothpaste	**pasta de dentes** *pah•stuh deh dehntz*

For Baby Essentials, see page 151.

The Basics

Grammar

In Brazilian Portuguese, there are three ways to say 'you' (taking different verb forms): **tu** and **você**.
However, in Brazil, **tu** is hardly ever used. **Tu** refers to just one person at a time, and it takes the second person singular form of the verb.
Você is predominantly used when talking to anyone, regardless of age or class. **Você(s)** takes either the third person singular or the third person plural of the verb depending on whether you're referring to one person (**você**) or more than one person (**vocês**).
The most formal way of saying 'you' is **o(s) senhor(es)** to a man (men) and **a(s) senhora(s)** to a woman (women). **O(s) senhor(es)** and **a(s) senhora(s)** take either the third person singular of the verb or the third person plural depending on whether you're referring to one person (**o senhor/a senhora**) or more than one person (**os senhores/as senhoras**).

Regular Verbs

Here are three of the main categories of regular verbs in the present tense:

	-ar falar (to speak)	-er comer (to eat)	-ir cobrir (to cover)
eu	**falo**	**como**	**cubro**
tu	**falas**	**comes**	**cobres**
ele/ela/você	**fala**	**come**	**cobre**
nós	**falamos**	**comemos**	**cobrimos**
vós	**falais**	**comeis**	**cobris**
eles/elas/vocês	**falam**	**comem**	**cobrem**

Irregular Verbs

In Brazilian Portuguese there are two main verbs meaning 'to be', both of which are irregular.

Ser indicates a permanent state:

Sou inglês. I'm English.

É portuguesa. She is Portuguese.

Estar indicates movement or a temporary state:

Está doente. He is sick [ill].

Estou passeando. I am walking.

Nouns & Articles

Nouns are either masculine or feminine. Masculine nouns usually end in **-o** and feminine nouns in **-a**. Normally nouns that end in a vowel become plural by adding an **-s**.

Articles must agree with the noun to which they refer in gender and number.

Indefinite: um carro (a car); **uns carros** (some cars); **uma casa** (a house); **umas** casas (some houses)

Definite: o carro (the cars); **os carros** (some cars); **a casa** (the house); **as casas** (the houses)

Word Order

The conjugated verb comes after the subject:

For example:

Maria fala inglês. Maria speaks English.

To ask a question, reverse the order of the subject and verb, change your intonation or use key question words such as **quando** (when).

Quando abre o museu? When does the museum open?

Literally translates to: 'When opens the museum?'

Ela é brasileira? Is she Brazilian?

Literally: She is Brazilian? This is a statement that becomes a question by raising the pitch of the last syllable of the sentence.

Negation

To form a negative sentence, add **não** (not) before the verb. E.g:

Fumamos. We smoke.

Não fumamos. We don't smoke.

Imperatives

Imperative sentences, commands, are formed by adding the appropriate ending to the stem of the verb.

For example:

Fale! Speak!

Abra a janela, por favor. Open the window, please.

Comparative & Superlative

The comparative is usually formed by adding **mais** (more) or **menos** (less) before the adjective or noun. The superlative is formed by adding the appropriate definite article (**o/os**, **a/as**) and **mais** (the most) or **menos** (the least).

alto	**mais alto**	**o mais alto**
tall	taller	tallest
caro	**menos caro**	**o menos caro**
expensive	less expensive	least expensive

Possessive Pronouns

Pronouns serve as substitutes for specific nouns and must agree with the noun in gender and number.

meu *m* /**minha** *f*	mine
teu *m* /**tua** *f*	yours
seu *m* /**sua** *f*	yours (formal)
nosso *m* /**nossa** *f*	ours
vosso *m* /**vossa** *f*	yours (plural)

E.g.: **Esse assento é meu.** That seat is mine.

Adjectives

Adjectives describe nouns and must agree with the noun in gender and number. In Brazilian Portuguese, adjectives usually come after the noun. Masculine adjectives usually end in **-o**, feminine adjectives in **-a**. If the masculine form ends in **-e** (**intellegente**) or with a consonant (**fácil**), the feminine form is generally the same.

For example:

Seu filho/Sua filha é agradável. Your son/daughter is nice.

O mar/A flor azul. The blue ocean/flower.

Adverbs & Adverbial Expressions

Adverbs are used to describe verbs. Some adverbs are formed by adding **-mente** to the singular feminine form of the adjective.

For example:

sincera + mente = sinceramente

The following are some common adverbial time expressions:

agora	now
ainda não	not yet
ainda	still
nunca	never
sempre	always

Numbers

ESSENTIAL

0	**zero** *zeh•roo*
1	**um** *m* **/uma** *f oong/oo•muh*
2	**dois** *m* **/duas** *f doyz/thoo•uhz*
3	**três** *trehz*
4	**quatro** *kwah•troo*
5	**cinco** *seeng•koo*
6	**seis** *sayz*
7	**sete** *seht*
8	**oito** *oy•too*
9	**nove** *nawv*
10	**dez** *dehz*
11	**onze** *aunz*
12	**doze** *dauz*
13	**treze** *trehz*
14	**catorze** *kuh•taurz*
15	**quinze** *keengz*
16	**dezesseis** *dehz•eh•sayz*
17	**dezessete** *dehz•eh•seht*
18	**dezoito** *dehz•oy•too*
19	**dezenove** *deh•zuh•nawv*
20	**vinte** *veent*
21	**vinte e um** *m* **/uma** *f veent ee oong/oo•muh*
22	**vinte e dois** *m* **/duas** *f veent ee doyz/thoo•uhz*
30	**trinta** *treeng•tuh*
31	**trinta e um** *m* **/uma** *f treeng•tuh ee oong/oo•muh*
40	**quarenta** *kwuh•rehn•tuh*
50	**cinquenta** *seeng•kwehn•tuh*

60	**sessenta** *seh•sehn•tuh*
70	**setenta** *seh•tehn•tuh*
80	**oitenta** *oy•tehn•tuh*
90	**noventa** *noo•vehn•tuh*
100	**cem** *sehn*
101	**cento e um** *m* **/uma** *f sehn•too ee oong/oo•muh*
200	**duzentos** *m* **/duzentas** *f doo•zehn•tooz/doo•zehn•tuhz*
500	**quinhentos** *m* **/quinhentas** *f kee•nyehn•tooz/ kee•nyehn•tuhz*
1,000	**mil** *meel*
10,000	**dez mil** *dehz meel*
1,000,000	**um milhão** *oong mee•lyohm*

Ordinal Numbers

first	**o primeiro** *m* **/a primeira** *f oo pree•may•roo/uh pree•may•ruh*
second	**o segundo** *m* **/a segunda** *f oo seh•goon•doo/uh seh•goon•duh*
third	**o terceiro** *m* **/a terceira** *f oo tehr•say•roo/uh tehr•say•ruh*
fourth	**o quarto** *m* **/a quarta** *f oo kwahr•too/uh kwahr•tuh*
fifth	**o quinto** *m* **/a quinta** *f oo keen•too/uh keen•tuh*
once	**uma vez** *oo•muh vehz*
twice	**duas vezes** *thoo•uhz veh•zehz*
three times	**três vezes** *trehz veh•zehz*

Brazilian Portuguese uses a comma for a decimal point and a period [full stop] or space for thousands, e.g. 4,95; 4.575.000 or 4 575 000.

Time

ESSENTIAL

What time is it?	**Por favor, que horas são?** *poor fuh•vaur keh aw•ruhz sohm*
It's noon [mid-day].	**É meio-dia.** *eh may•oo dee•uh*
At midnight.	**À meia-noite.** *ah may•uh noyt*
From nine o'clock to five o'clock.	**Das nove às cinco horas.** *duhz nawv ahz seeng•koo aw•ruhz*
Twenty [after] past four.	**Quatro e vinte.** *kwah•troo ee veent*
A quarter to nine.	**Quinze para as nove.** *kinz puh•ruh uhz nawv*
5:30 a.m./p.m.	**Cinco e meia de manhã/da tarde.** *seeng•koo ee may•uh deh muh•nyuh/duh tahrd*

In Brazil, time is usually written using the 24-hour clock, e.g. "The movie starts at 17:00". However, when speaking, use the 12-hour clock. For example, 1:00 p.m. is not 13:00 but "**uma hora da tarde**".

Days

ESSENTIAL

Monday	**segunda-feira** *seh•goon•duh fay•ruh*
Tuesday	**terça-feira** *tehr•suh fay•ruh*
Wednesday	**quarta-feira** *kwahr•tuh fay•ruh*
Thursday	**quinta-feira** *keen•tuh fay•ruh*
Friday	**sexta-feira** *say•stuh fay•ruh*
Saturday	**sábado** *sah•buh•thoo*
Sunday	**domingo** *doo•meeng•goo*

In Brazil, calendars go from Monday to Sunday. When giving dates, give the day first, then the month, then the year (e.g. 1 May 2009 or 1/5/2014).

Dates

yesterday	**ontem** *awn•teng*
today	**hoje** *auzseh*
tomorrow	**amanhã** *uh•muh•nuh*
day	**o dia** *oo dee•uh*
week	**a semana** *uh seh•muh•nuh*
month	**o mês** *oo mehz*
year	**o ano** *oo uh•noo*

Months

January	**Janeiro** *zher•nay•roo*
February	**Fevereiro** *feh•vray•roo*
March	**Março** *mahr•soo*
April	**Abril** *uh•breel*
May	**Maio** *meye•oo*
June	**Junho** *zsoo•nyoo*
July	**Julho** *zsoo•lyoo*
August	**Agosto** *uh•gaus•too*
September	**Setembro** *seh•tehm•broo*
October	**Outubro** *aw•too•broo*
November	**Novembro** *noo•vehm•broo*
December	**Dezembro** *deh•zehm•broo*

Seasons

the spring	**a primavera** *uh pree•muh•veh•ruh*
the summer	**o verão** *oo vrohm*
the fall [autumn]	**o outono** *oo aw•too•noo*
the winter	**o inverno** *oo eeng•verr•noo*

The dates of **Carnaval** are based on the dates of Lent and Easter, and therefore change every year. **Carnaval** starts on the Saturday before Ash Wednesday and lasts until Ash Wednesday.

Holidays

January 1	New Year's Day
January 6	Epiphany
April 11	Tiradentes Day
May 1	May Day
August 15	Assumption Day
September 7	Independence Day
October 1	Our Lady of Aparecida Day
November 1	All Saints' Day
November 15	Proclamation Day
December 8	Immaculate Conception Day
December 25	Christmas Day

Conversion Tables

When you know	Multiply by	To find
ounces	28.3	grams
pounds	0.45	kilograms
inches	2.54	centimeters
feet	0.3	meters
miles	1.61	kilometers
square inches	6.45 sq.	centimeters
square feet	0.09 sq.	meters
square miles	2.59 sq.	kilometers
pints (U.S./Brit)	0.47/0.56	liters
gallons (U.S./Brit)	3.8/4.5	liters
Fahrenheit	5/9, after 32	Centigrade
Centigrade	9/5, then +32	Fahrenheit

Kilometers to Miles Conversions

1 km – 0.62 mi	**20 km** – 12.4 mi
5 km – 3.10 mi	**50 km** – 31.0 mi
10 km – 6.20 mi	**100 km** – 61.0 mi

Measurement

1 gram	**grama**	= 0.035 oz.
1 kilogram (kg)	**quilo**	= 2.2 lb
1 liter (l)	**litro**	= 1.06 U.S/0.88 Brit. quarts
1 centimeter (cm)	**centimetro**	= 0.4 inch
1 meter (m)	**metro**	= 3.28 ft.
1 kilometer (km)	**quilômetro**	= 0.62 mile

Temperature

-40° C – -40° F	**-1° C** – 30° F	**20° C** – 68° F
-30° C – -22° F	**0° C** – 32° F	**25° C** – 77° F
-20° C – -4° F	**5° C** – 41° F	**30° C** – 86° F
-10° C – 14° F	**10° C** – 50° F	**35° C** – 95° F
-5° C – 23° F	**15° C** – 59° F	

Oven Temperature

100° C – 212° F	**149° C** – 300° F	**204° C** – 400° F
121° C – 250° F	**177° C** – 350° F	**260° C** – 500° F

Dictionary

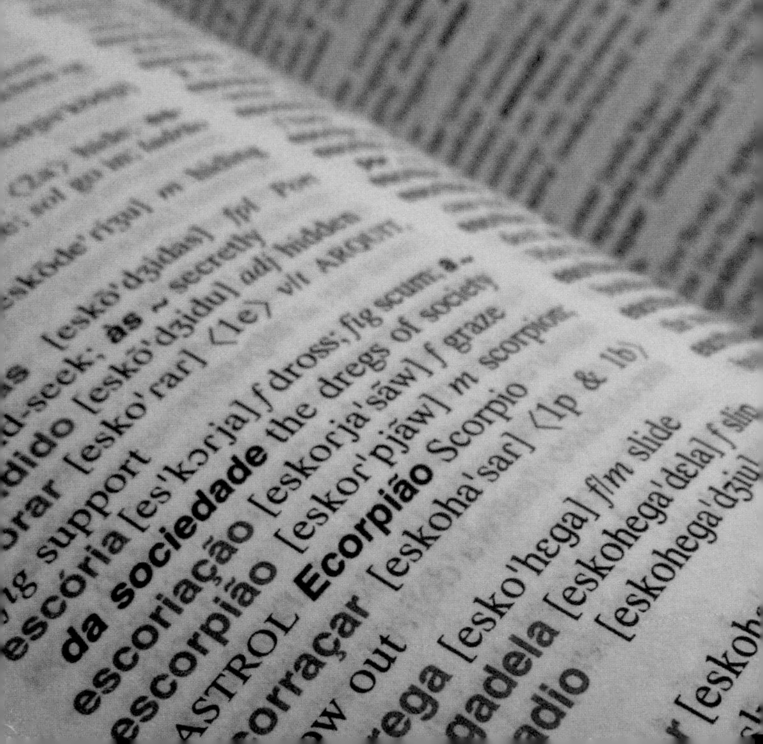

English–Brazilian Portuguese

A

abbey a abadia
able capaz
about a cerca de
above acima
abroad no exterior
abscess o abcesso
accept aceitar
access o acesso
accident o acidente
accidentally sem querer
accommodation o alojamento
accompany acompanhar
accountant contador
activity a atividade
across do outro lado
adaptor o adaptador
address o endereço
admission charge o preço de entrada
adult o adulto
aerobics aeróbica
after depois
afternoon tarde
aftershave a loção pós barba
after-sun lotion a loção pós-sol
age a idade
ago há
agree concordar
air conditioning o ar condicionado
air mattress o colchão pneumático [o colchão de ar]
air pump a máquina pneumática [a bomba de ar]
airline a linha aérea
airmail o correio aéreo
airport o aeroporto
aisle seat o assento de corredor
alarm clock o despertador
alcoholic drink a bebida alcoólica
all tudo
allergic alérgico
allergy a alergia
allow permitir
almost quase
alone sózinho
already já
also também
alter modificar
alternate route o caminho

adj adjective
adv adverb
BE British English
n noun
prep preposition
v verb

alternativo
aluminum foil o papel alumínio
always sempre
ambassador o embaixador
ambulance a ambulância
American o americano, a americana
anesthetic a anestesia
and e
announcement anúncio
another outro, outra
answer atender [responder]
antibiotic o antibiótico
antifreeze o anticongelante
antique a antiguidade
antiseptic cream a pomada antiséptica
any algum
anyone else mais alguém
anyone alguém
anything alguma coisa
apartment o apartamento
apologize pedir desculpa
apology a desculpa
appointment a consulta
approximately aproximadamente
archery arco e flecha
architect o arquiteto, a arquiteta
architecture a arquitetura
area a área
area code o código de área
around (the corner) ao virar a esquina
arrange arranjar
arrivals (airport) chegadas
arrive chegar
art a arte
art gallery a galeria de arte
artificial sweetener o adoçante
artist o/a artista
ashtray o cinzeiro
ask pedir
asleep adormecido, adormecida
aspirin a aspirina
at least pelo menos
athletics atletismo
attack o ataque
attendant o empregado, a empregada
attractive atraente
aunt a tia
Australia a Austrália
Australian o australiano, a australiana
authentic autêntico
authenticity autenticidade
automatic (car) o carro de câmbio automático
automatic teller machine (ATM) o caixa eletrênico
avalanche a avalanche
away longe
awful horrível

B

baby o bebê [neném]; **~sitter** baby-sitter [a babá]; **~wipes** os lenços umedecidos para o bebê [neném]
baby bottle a mamadeira
back as costas
backache a dor de costas
backpack a mochila
bacon toucinho
bad mau, má
bakery a padaria
balcony a varanda
ball a bola
ballet o ballet [o balé]
band (musical) a banda musical
bandage a atadura
bank o banco
bar o bar
barber o barbeiro
baseball beisebol
basement o porão
basin a bacia
basket o cesto
basketball basquetebol
bath a banheira
bathe tomar banho
bathroom o banheiro
battery a pilha; **~ (car, computer)** a bateria
battle site o campo de batalha
be *v* ser; **~ (temporary state)** estar; **~ (location)** ficar
beach a praia
beard a barba
beautiful bonito, bonita
because porque; **~ of** por causa de
bed a cama; **~ and breakfast** pousada [pernoite e café da manhã]
bedding a roupa de cama
bedroom o quarto (de dormir)
bee a abelha
beer a cerveja
before antes de
begin *v* começar
beginner o/a principiante
beginning o começo
beige beige [bege]
belong pertencer
belt o cinto
best melhor
better melhor
between entre
bib o babador
bicycle a bicicleta
big grande
bigger o/a maior
bikini o biquini
binoculars os binóculos
bird o pássaro
bishop o bispo
bite (insect) a picada (de inseto)

bitter azedo
bizarre estranho
black preto
blanket o cobertor
bleach alvejante
blouse a blusa
blow-dry o secador
blue azul
blueberry o mirtilo
board embarcar
boarding (plane) embarque
boarding pass cartão de embarque
boat o barco
boiled cozido
book *n* o livro
book *v* reservar
book of tickets a caderneta de bilhetes
bookstore a livraria
boots as botas
border a fronteira
boring entediante
botanical garden o jardim botânico
bottle a garrafa; **~ opener** o abridor de garrafas
bowl a tijela
box office a bilheteria
boxing o boxe
boy o menino
boyfriend o namorado
bra o sutiã
bracelet a pulseira
brake *n* o freio
brass o latão
Brazil o Brasil
Brazilian brasileiro
bread o pão
break *v* partir [quebrar]
breakdown avariar [quebrar]
break-in o assalto
breakfast o café da manhã
breathe *v* respirar
bridge a ponte
briefcase a maleta
briefs as calcinhas
brilliant brilhante
bring *v* trazer
Britain a Grã-Bretanha
British britânico
brochure o folheto
bronze o bronze
brother o irmão
brown o castanho
brush a escova
bucket (pail) o balde
build *v* construir
building o edifício
built construído
burger o hambúrguer
burglary o roubo
burnt queimado

bus o ônibus; **~ (long-distance)** o ônibus; **~ station** a estação rodoviária; **~ stop** a parada de ônibus
business class (na) classe executiva;
~ a trip viagem de negócios
business card o cartão de visitas
busy ocupado
but mas
butcher shop o açougue
butter a manteiga
button o botão
buy *v* comprar
bye adeus [tchau]

C

cabin a cabine [o camarote]
cable car o funicular; o teleférico
café o café
cake o bolo
calendar o calendário
call *v* chamar
camcorder a câmera de vídeo
camera a máquina fotográfica; **~ case** o estojo para a máquina; **~ store** a loja de artigos fotográficos
camp *v* acampar
camping campismo [camping]; **~ equipment** o material de campismo [camping]
campsite o parque de campismo [camping]
can *n* a lata; **~ opener** o abridor de latas
Canadá o Canadá
Canadian canadense
canal o canal
cancel *v* cancelar
cancer (disease) o câncer
candle a vela
candy os doces [as balas]
canoe a canoa
canoeing fazer canoagem
canyon o desfiladeiro
car o carro; **~ hire [BE]** aluguel de carros; **~ park [BE]** o parque de estacionamento;
~ rental aluguel de carros
carafe a jarra
card o cartão ; **ATM ~** o cartão eletrônico; **credit ~** o cartão de crédito; **debit ~** o cartão de débito; **phone ~** o cartão de telefônico
cards as cartas
carpet o tapete
carry transportar
carry-on levar
carton o pacote
cash o dinheiro

cash *v* cobrar
casino o casino
castle o castelo
cat o gato [a gata]
catch *v* **(bus)** apanhar o ônibus
cathedral a catedral
cause *v* causar
cave a caverna
CD o CD
CD-player CD-player, o leitor de CDs
cell phone o celular
celcius celsius
cemetery o cemitério
cent o centavo
certificate o certificado
chair a cadeira
change *n* **(coins)** troco (moeda); ~ *v* **(bus)** mudar (de ônibus); ~ *v* **(clothes)** trocar (de roupa); ~ *v* **(money)** trocar dinheiro; ~ *v* **(reservation)** mudar a reserva
changing rooms os vestiários
channel (sea) o canal
chapel a capela
charcoal o carvão
charge a tarifa
cheap barato
cheaper mais barato
check (bill) a conta; **put it on the ~** ponha na conta
check *v* verificar
checkbook o talão de cheques
check-in desk o balcão de registro
check out *v* **(hotel)** pagar a conta
checking account a conta corrente
checkout (supermarket) o caixa
cheers saúde
cheese o queijo
chemical toilet banheiro químico
chemist [BE] a farmácia
chickenpox a varicela
child a criança
child's seat a cadeirinha de criança; ~ **(in car)** a cadeira de criança
chips [BE] as batatas fritas
church a igreja
cigarette o cigarro
cigars os charutos
cinema o cinema
class a classe
clean *adj* limpo [limpa]
clean *v* limpar
cleaner (person) o empregado da limpeza; ~ **(product)** o produto de limpeza
cliff a falésia
cling film [BE] o papel aderente
clock o relógio
close (near) perto
close *v* fechar
clothes a roupa; ~ **dryer** a

máquina de secar
clothing store a loja de artigos de vestuário
cloudy nublado
clubs (golf) os tacos de golfe
coast a costa
coat o casaco [comprido]
cockroach a barata
coffee o café
coin a moeda
cold frio; ~ **(illness)** o resfriado
colleague o colega
college o colégio
color a cor
comb o pente
comedy a comédia
comforter o edredom
commission a comissão
compartment (train) o compartimento
compass o compasso; a bússola
complain reclamar
complaint a reclamação
computer o computador
conditioner (hair) o condicionador para o cabelo
condom o preservativo
conductor (orchestra) o maestro
conference a conferência
confirm *v* confirmar
confirmation a confirmação
connect conectar
connection (flight) conexão
conscious consciente
constipation a prisão de ventre
consulate o consulado
contact *v* contatar
contact lens as lentes de contacto
contain *v* conter
contageous contagioso
contraceptive o contraceptivo; anticoncepcional
convenient conveniente
cook o cozinheiro, a cozinheira
cook *v* cozinhar
cool (temperature) fresco
copper o cobre
corkscrew o saca-rolhas
corn o milho
corner a esquina
correct correto
cost o custo
cot a cama de bebê [neném], o berço
cotton o algodão
cough *n* a tosse; ~ *v* tossir
country (nation) o país
countryside o campo
couple (pair) o par
course (meal) o prato
cousin o primo [a prima]
crash *n* **(car)** a batida [o acidente]

credit card o cartão de crédito; **~ number** o número do cartão de crédito
cross *v* **(road)** atravessar
crowded lotado; com muita gente
cruise o cruzeiro
crystal o cristal
cup a xícara
cupboard o armário
currency a moeda
currency exchange (office) casa de câmbio
customs a alfândega; **~ declaration** declaração da alfândega
cut *n* o corte; **~** *v* cortar
cycling [BE] o ciclismo

D

daily diariamente
damage danificado
damp úmido
dance *n* a dança; **~** *v* dançar; **~ club** o clube de dança
dangerous perigoso
dark escuro
daughter filha
dawn a madrugada
day o dia
dead morto; **~ (battery)** descarregada
deaf surdo
debit card (Port) o cartão de débito
deck chair espreguiçadeira
declare *v* declarar
decline o declínio
deduct *v* **(money)** deduzir
deep profundo
degrees (temperature) os graus
delay o atraso
delete (computer) apagar
delicatessen a loja de conveniência
delicious delicioso
deliver *v* entregar
denim o jeans [brim]
dental floss o fio dental
dentist o dentista
deodorant o desodorante
depart *v* **(train, bus)** partida
department store loja de departamentos
departure (train) a partida
depend depende
deposit *n* o depósito
deposit *v* depositar
destination o destino
detergent detergente
diabetes o diabetes
diabetic o diabético
diamonds os diamantes
diaper a fralda

diarrhea a diarreia
dictionary o dicionário
diesel o diesel
difficult difícil
digital digital
dining room a sala de jantar
dinner o jantar
direct *adj* direto
direct *v* indicar
direction a direção
directory (telephone) a lista telefônica
dirty sujo, suja
disabled (person) o/a deficiente
disconnect (computer) desligar [desconectar]
discount o desconto
dish (meal) o prato
dishes a louça
dishwashing liquid o detergente para a louça
display case a vitrine
disposable (camera) máquina descartável
dive *v* mergulhar
divorced divorciado
doctor o médico
dog o cão
doll a boneca
dollar (U.S.) o dólar
domestic (flight) doméstico
door a porta
double bed a cama de casal
double room o quarto de casal
down abaixo
downstairs em baixo
downtown o centro da cidade
dozen dúzia
dress *n* **(clothing)** vestido
drink *n* bebida
drinking water água potável
drive *v* conduzir
driver condutor
driver's license a carteira de motorista
drugstore a farmácia
drunk o bêbado
dry cleaner a lavanderia de limpeza a seco
during durante
dusty empoeirado
duty (tax) imposto
duty-free goods a mercadoria isenta de impostos
duty-free shopping as compras duty-free

E

ear o ouvido
ear drops gotas para os ouvidos
earlier mais cedo
early cedo

earrings os brincos
east leste
easy fácil
eat comer
economy class a classe econômica
electricity a eletricidade
elevator o elevador
e-mail *n* o email; *v* enviar e-mails
e-mail address endereço de e-mail
embassy a embaixada
emerald a esmeralda
emergency a emergência;
  ~ exit a saída de emergência
empty *adj* vazio [vazia]
enamel (jewelry) esmaltaldo
end *v* terminar
engine o motor
England a Inglaterra
English inglês
enjoy *v* apreciar
enough bastante [suficiente]
enter entrar
entertainment entretenimento
envelope o envelope
equipment (sports) o equipamento (esportivo)
erase *v* apagar
error o erro
escalator a escada rolante
essential essencial
e-ticket o bilhete electrônico
EU (European Union) a UE (União Europeia)
euro o euro
Europe a Europa
except exceto
excess o excesso
exchange *v* trocar
exchange rate a taxa de câmbio
excursion a excursão
excuse me (apology) desculpe-me; **(to get attention)** com licença
exhausted *adj* exausto [exausta]
exhibition a exposição
exit a saída
expensive caro
expiration date a data de validade
extremely extremamente
eye o olho

F

face a cara; o rosto
facial a limpeza de pele
family a família
famous famoso
fan (electric) o ventilador
far longe
fare o bilhete
farm a fazenda
fast depressa
faster mais rápido

fast food as refeições rápidas
fat *n* a gordura; *adj* gordo
fat-free sem gordura
father o pai
faucet a torneira
favorite o preferido, a preferida
fax *n* o fax
fax *v* enviar fax
fear o medo
feed *v* alimentar
female a mulher
ferry a balsa
few poucos
fever a febre
field (sports) o campo
fill out *v* **(form)** preencher
film (camera) o filme
fine (penalty) a multa
fire *n* o fogo
fire alarm o alarme de incêndio
fire department [brigade] o corpo de bombeiros
fire escape a saída de incêndio
fire extinguisher o extintor de incêndio
first o primeiro
first class a primeira classe
first-aid kit o estojo de primeiros socorros
fit (clothes) servir
fitting room o provador
fix *v* consertar
flag a bandeira
flash (photography) o flash
flashlight a lanterna
flat (tire) o furo (no pneu)
flight o vôo
floor (level) o andar
flower a flor
fly (insect) a mosca
fly *v* voar
food a comida
football [BE] o futebol
forecast a previsão
foreign o estrangeiro; **~ currency** as moedas estrangeiras
forest a floresta
forget *v* esquecer
fork (utensil) o garfo; **~ (in road)** a bifurcação
form o formulário
formula (baby) a papa
fortunately felizmente
fountain a fonte
free (available) livre; **~ (no charge)** grátis
frequently muitas vezes, frequentemente
fresh fresco
friend o amigo, a amiga
full cheio
furniture a mobília; os móveis

G

gallon o galão
game o jogo
garage a garagem [a oficina mecânica]
garbage bag o saco de lixo
garden o jardim
gardener o jardineiro
gasoline a gasolina
gate (airport) o portão
gay club o clube gay
genuine autêntico, autêntica
get out *v* sair
gift a oferta
girl a menina
girlfriend a namorada
give *v* dar
give way (on the road) [BE] dar prioridade
glass (drinking) o copo
glass (material) o vidro
glove a luva
go ir
golf o golfe
good bom [boa]; **~ morning** bom dia; **~night** boa noite
goodbye adeus
gram o grama
grandparent o avô, a avó
grape a uva
gray o cinza
green o verde
grocery store a mercearia
ground (camping) o terreno
group o grupo
guarantee a garantia
guide (person) o/a guia
guidebook o guia

H

hair o cabelo; **~ gel** o gel para o cabelo; **~brush** a escova de cabelo; **~dryer** o secador de cabelo; **~spray** o spray para o cabelo
haircut o corte de cabelo
hairdresser (ladies/men) o cabeleireiro (senhoras/homens)
half metade
hammer o martelo
hand a mão
hand cream o creme para as mãos
hand luggage [BE] a bagagem de mão
handbag [BE] a bolsa
handicapped o/a deficiente
handicapped accessible acessível a deficientes
hangover a ressaca
happy feliz
hat o chapéu
have *v* ter

head a cabeça
health a saúde
hear *v* ouvir
hearing aid o aparelho auditivo
heater o aquecedor
heating [BE] aquecimento
heavy pesado
height a altura
hello oi, olá
help *n* a ajuda
help *v* ajudar
here aqui
high alto(a)
high tide a maré alta
highway a rodovia
hike (walk) o passeio a pé
hiking caminhada
hill a colina
hire *v* **[BE]** alugar
hire car [BE] o carro de aluguel
hitchhike *v* pedir carona
hitchhiking viajar de carona
hold *v* **(contain)** conter
holiday o feriado
holiday [BE] as férias
home a casa
horse o cavalo
horseracing a corrida de cavalos
hospital o hospital
hostel o albergue
hot (temperature) quente; **(spicy)** picante
hot spring a nascente de água quente
hot water a água quente
hotel o hotel
hour a hora
house a casa
household goods os artigos para a casa
how (question) como
how much (question) quanto
hurt *adj* o ferido, a ferida
husband o marido

I

ice o gelo
ice cream o sorvete; **~ parlor** a sorveteria; **~ cone** o cone de sorvete
ice hockey o hóquei no gelo
icy *adj* gelado, gelada
identification a identificação
ill *adj* o/a doente
illness a doença
in (place) no; **(time)** em
indoor dentro de casa; **~ pool** a piscina coberta
inexpensive barato
inflammation a inflamação
informal (dress) (o vestido) informal

information a informação
innocent o/a inocente
insect o inseto; **~ bite** a picada de inseto; **~ repellent** o repelente de insetos
inside dentro de
insomnia a insônia
instant coffee o café instantâneo
instant message a mensagem instantânea
insulin a insulina
insurance o seguro; **~ card** a apólice de seguro
interesting interessante
international internacional
internet cafe o cyber café
internet service o serviço de internet
interpreter o/a intérprete
intersection o cruzamento
introduce *v* introduzir
invite *v* convidar
Ireland a Irlanda
Irish irlandês
iron *v* passar a ferro
island a ilha

J

jam geleia
jar o frasco
jeans as calças jeans
jellyfish a água-viva
jewelry as joias
joke a piada
judge o juiz, a juíza
jumper cables os cabos da bateria

K

key a chave
key card o cartão da porta
kiddie pool a piscina de bebês [nenens]
kilo(gram) o quilo(grama)
kilometer o quilometro
kiosk o quiosque
kiss beijar
kitchen a cozinha
knee o joelho

L

lace a renda
ladder a escada
lake o lago
large grande
last o último
late (time) tarde; **(delayed)** atrasado
later mais tarde
launderette [BE] lavanderia automática
laundromat lavanderia automática
laundry service o serviço de

lavanderia
lawyer o advogado, a advogada
learn *v* aprender
leather o couro
leave *v* partir
left a esquerda
left-luggage office [BE] o depósito de bagagem
lens lentes
less menos
lesson a lição
letter a carta
library a biblioteca
life a vida
lifeboat o barco salva-vidas
lifeguard o salva-vidas
life jacket o colete salva-vidas
lift [BE] o elevador
light (shade) claro; **(weight)** leve
light *n* a luz; *v* ascender
lightbulb a lâmpada (elétrica)
lighter o isqueiro
lightning o relâmpago
line (waiting) a fila (de espera)
line (subway) a linha (do metrô)
linen o linho
lip o lábio
liquor store a loja de bebidas alcoólicas
liter o litro
little pequeno, pequena
live *v* viver
local regional
lock *n* a fechadura
locked *adj* fechado, fechada
locker o armário com cadeado
log on *v* autenticar
log off *v* sair
long comprido; **(time)** muito
long-sighted [BE] hipermetrope
look *v* ver
look for procurar
lose *v* perder
lost *adj* perdido
lost-and-found os achados e perdidos
lotion a loção
louder mais alto
love (a person) amar; **(a thing)** gostar de
luggage a bagagem
luggage cart [trolley] o carrinho
luggage locker o guarda-volumes (debagagem)
luggage ticket o cacnhoto do guarda-volumes (de bagagem)
lumpy (mattress) (o colchão) desnivelado
lunch o almoço
lung o pulmão

M

magazine a revista
magnificent magnífico, magnífica
mail o correio
mailbox a caixa do correio
main course o prato principal
make up a prescription [BE] receitar
male masculino
man o homem
manager o/a gerente
manicure a manicure
manual (gears) câmbio manual (de marchas)
market o mercado
married casado
mass (church service) a missa
massage a massagem
matches (fire) os fósforos
material o material
mattress o colchão
maybe talvez
meal a refeição
mean *v* significar
measure *v* medir
measurement a medida
meat a carne
medicine o remédio
medium (size) médio; **(cooked)** ao ponto
meet *v* encontrar(-se)
mend *v* consertar
menu o menu, o cardápio
message a mensagem
metal o metal
meter (taxi) o taxímetro
meter (parking) o parquímetro
microwave (oven) o microondas
midday [BE] o meio-dia
migraine a enxaqueca
mileage a quilometragem
minibar o frigobar
minute o minuto
mirror o espelho
miss *v* perder
missing em falta
mistake o engano, o erro
misunderstanding o mal-entendido
mobile phone [BE] o celular
mobile home a casa ambulante
modern moderno, moderna
money o dinheiro
monument o monumento
moped a mobilete
more mais
mosquito o mosquito
mother a mãe
motion sickness o enjôo
motor o motor
motorbike a moto
motorboat o barco a motor, a

lancha
motorway [BE] a estrada, a rodovia
mountain a montanha; **~ bike** mountain bike
moustache o bigode
mouth a boca
move *v* mudar(-se)
movie o filme
movie theater o cinema
much muito
mug (drinking) a caneca
mugging o assalto
mumps a caxumba
museum o museu
music a música

N

nail (body) a unha; **~polish** o esmalte de unhas
name o nome
napkin o guardanapo
nappy [BE] a fralda
narrow estreito
national nacional
nationality a nacionalidade
nature preserve a reserva natural
nausea a náusea
near perto
nearest mais próximo
necessary necessário
neck (body) o pescoço; **(clothing)** a gola
necklace o colar
needle a agulha
neighbor o vizinho, a vizinha
nephew o sobrinho
never nunca
new novo, nova
newspaper o jornal
newsstand [newsagent] a banca de jornais
next próximo, próxima
next to ao lado de
niece a sobrinha
night a noite
nightclub o nightclub
no não
no one ninguém
noisy barulhento
non-alcoholic não-alcoólico, não-alcoólica
non-smoking *adj* não-fumantes
none nenhum, nenhuma
normal normal
north o norte
note a nota
note [BE] a nota
notebook o caderno
nothing nada
now agora
number (telephone) o número de telefone

number plate (car) [BE] a placa do carro
nurse o enfermeiro, a enfermeira

O

observatory o observatório
occupied ocupado, ocupada
off-licence [BE] a loja de vinhos
office o escritório
often muitas vezes
oil o óleo
okay O.K.
old o velho, a velha
old-fashioned antigo, antiga
one um, uma
one-way ticket o bilhete de ida
open *v* abrir
open *adj* aberto, aberta
opening hours as horas de funcionamento
opera a ópera
operation a operação
opposite o oposto
optician o oculista, oftalmologista
orange (fruit) a laranja; **(color)** laranja
orchestra a orquestra
order *v* encomendar
outdoor ao ar livre; **~ pool** a piscina ao ar livre
outside fora de
over sobre
overdone *adj* cozido demais
overnight só uma noite

P

pacifier a chupeta
pack *v* fazer as malas
package o pacote
paddling pool [BE] a piscina de bebês [nenens]
padlock o cadeado
pain a dor
paint *v* pintar
painter o pintor, a pintora
painting o quadro
pajamas o pijama
palace o palácio
pants as calças
pantyhose a meia-calça
paper o papel
paper napkin o guardanapo de papel
park o parque
park *v* estacionar
parking o estacionamento; **~ lot** o parque de estacionamento; **~ meter** o parquímetro; **~ space** a vaga de estacionamento
partner o companheiro, a companheira
part a peça

party a festa
pass *n* o passe
pass *v* passar
passenger o passageiro, a passageira
passport o passaporte
pastry shop a doceria [a confeitaria]
patch *v* remendar
path o caminho
pay *v* pagar
pay phone o telefone público
peak (mountain) o pico
pearl a pérola
pedestrian crossing a faixa de pedestres
pedicure a pedicure
pen a caneta
pencil o lápis
penicillin a penicilina
per por: ~ **day** por dia; ~ **hour** por hora; ~ **night** por noite; ~ **week** por semana
performance a sessão
perfume o perfume
perhaps talvez
period período
permit a permissão; *v* permitir
petrol [BE] a gasolina; ~ **station [BE]** o posto de gasolina
pharmacy a farmácia
phone o telefone; ~ **call** o telefonema; ~ **card** o cartão telefônico
photo a fotografia
photocopier a fotocopiadora
photographer o fotógrafo, a fotógrafa
photography a fotografia
pick up *v* ir buscar; **(collect)** levantar
picnic o piquenique; ~ **area** a área para piqueniques
piece a peça
pill (birth control) a pílula
pillow a almofada
personal identification number (PIN) o PIN
pink cor-de-rosa
piste [BE] a pista; ~ **map [BE]** o mapa de pistas
pizzeria a pizzaria
place o lugar; **(a bet)** apostar
plane o avião
plant a planta
plastic wrap o papel aderente
plate o prato
platform [BE] a plataforma
platinum a platina
play *v* jogar; **(instrument)** tocar
please por favor
plug (electric) a tomada (eléctrica)

plunger o desentupidor
pocket o bolso
poison o veneno
police a polícia; **~ report** o boletim de ocorrência da polícia; **~ station** a delegacia da polícia
pond a lagoa
pool a piscina
pop music a música pop
popcorn as pipocas
popular popular
port (harbor) o porto
Portugal Portugal
Portuguese português
post [BE] o correio; **~ office** os correios
postbox [BE] a caixa do correio
postcard o cartão postal
poster o pôster
pottery a cerâmica
pound (British sterling) a libra (esterlina)
pregnant a grávida
prescribe receitar
prescription a receita
press *v* **(clothing)** passar a ferro [engomar]
pretty bonito, bonita
print *v* imprimir
problem o problema
prohibit proibido
pronounce *v* pronunciar
public o público
pull *v* puxar
pump a bomba; **(gas)** a bomba de gasolina
puncture [BE] o furo

Q

quality a qualidade
question a pergunta
queue [BE] *n* a fila
quiet sossegado, sossegada

R

race (cars, horses) a corrida; **~ track** o hipódromo
racket (sports) a raquete
railway station [BE] a estação de caminhos de ferro [a estação ferroviária]
rain *v* chover
raincoat a capa de chuva
rape o estupro
rare (unusual) raro, rara; **(steak)** mal-passado, mal-passada
razor a navalha; **~ blade** a lâmina de barbear
read *v* ler
ready pronto, pronta
real (genuine) legítimo, legítima

receipt a fatura [o recibo]
reception (desk) a recepção
receptionist o/a recepcionista
recommend *v* recomendar
red vermelho, vermelha
refrigerator a geladeira
region a região
regular (gas/petrol) normal
rent *v* alugar
rental car o carro alugado
repair *v* arranjar
repeat *v* repetir
reservation a marcação
reserve *v* reservar
restaurant o restaurante
restroom o banheiro
return *v* **(come back)** voltar; **(give back)** devolver
right (correct) certo; **~ of way** prioridade
ring o anel
river o rio
road a estrada
robbed roubado, roubada
robbery o roubo
romantic romântico
room o quarto; **~ service** o serviço de quarto
round redondo, redonda
round-trip de ida e volta
route o caminho
rowboat o barco a remos
rubbish [BE] o lixo; **~ bin [BE]** a lata de lixo, lixeira
ruins as ruínas

S

sad triste
safe *n* o cofre; *adj* seguro
safety a segurança
sales tax IVA
same o mesmo, a mesma
sand a areia
sandals as sandálias
sanitary napkin [pad] o papel higiênica
saucepan a panela
sauna o sauna
save guardar
savings account a conta de poupança
scanner o scanner
scarf o lenço , a echarpe (de pescoço)
schedule o horário
school a escola
scissors a tesoura
sea o mar
seat o lugar
see ver
self-service self-service [auto-serviço]

sell *v* vender
send *v* mandar
senior citizen o idoso, a idosa
separated separado, separada
serious sério, séria
service charge a taxa de serviço
set menu o menu fixo
sex o sexo
sexually transmitted disease (STD) Doença Sexualmente Transmissível (DST)
shallow pouco fundo, funda
shampoo o shampoo [o xampú]
sharp afiado, afiada
shaving cream o creme da barba
sheet o lençol
ship o navio
shirt a camisa
shoe o sapato; **~ store** a sapataria
shopping compras; **~ area** a zona comercial; **~ centre [BE]** o centro comercial; **~ mall** o shopping center
short curto
shorts os calções
short sighted [BE] míope
show *n* o espectáculo; *v* mostrar
shower o chuveiro
sick doente
side (of road) o lado; **~effect** o efeito colateral; **~ order** à parte; **~ street** transversal
sidewalk a calçada
sightseeing tour o circuito turístico
sign o sinal
silk a seda
silver a prata
single (not married) solteiro; **~ room** o quarto individual
sink a pia
sister a irmã
sit *v* sentar
size o número/tamanho
skin a pele
skirt a saia
skis os esquis
sleep dormir
sleeping bag o saco de dormir
sleeper car [BE] vagão-leito
slice a fatia
slippers chinelos
slope (ski) a rampa
slow lento, lenta
slower mais devagar
slowly devagar
small pequeno, pequena
small change troco
smoke *v* fumar
smoking (area) zona de fumantes

snack bar a lanchonete, a cafetaria
sneakers os tênis
snorkel mergulho, snorkel
snow a neve; *v* nevar
snowboard a prancha de snowboard
soap o sabonete
soccer o futebol
sock a meia
soft drink (soda) o refrigerante
sold out esgotada, esgotado
someone alguém
something alguma coisa
sometimes às vezes
son o filho
sore throat a dor de garganta
sorry desculpe
south sul
souvenir a lembrança
spa o spa
speak falar
speed limit o limite de velocidade
speed *v* ir com excesso de velocidade
spell soletrar
spend gastar
spine a espinha
sponge a esponja
sport o esporte
sporting goods store a loja de esportivos
spring a primavera
square o quadrado
stadium o estádio
stairs as escadas
stamp o selo
start começar
starter [BE] a entrada; o aperitivo
station a estação
station wagon a minivan
statue a estátua
stay permanecer
steal roubar
steep íngreme
sting a picada
stolen roubado
stomach o estômago
stop *n* **(bus, tram)** a parada
stop *v* parar
store guide a planta da loja
storey [BE] o andar (do prédio)
straight ahead sempre em frente
stream o riacho
street a estrada
stroller o carrinho de bebê [neném]
student o/a estudante
study *v* estudar
subway o metrô; ~ **station** a estação de metrô
suit o terno
suitcase a mala de viagem

sun o sol
sun block o protetor solar
sunbathe tomar banho de sol
sunburn a queimadura de sol
sunglasses os óculos de sol
super (fuel) super
supermarket o supermercado
surfboard a prancha de surf
sweatshirt o agasalho, a blusa de moleton
sweet (taste) doce
sweets [BE] os doces, as balas
swim *v* nadar
swimsuit o maiô de banho
symbol o símbolo
synagogue a sinagoga

T

table a mesa
tablet (medicine) o comprimido
take *v* **(carry)** levar; **(medicine)** tomar; **(time)** demorar
take away [BE] para levar
tampons os tampões higiênicos
taste *v* provar
taxi o táxi; **~ stand** o ponto de táxis
team o time
teaspoon a colher de chá
telephone o telefone
tennis o tênis
tent a tenda; **~ peg** a cavilha; **~ pole** a estaca
terminal (airport) o terminal
text *v* **(send a message)** escrever uma mensagem; *n* **(message)** mensagem de texto
thank you obrigado m; obrigada f
that esse, essa
theater teatro
theft roubo
there ali
thief ladrão
thigh coxa
thirsty com sede
this este, esta
throat a garganta
ticket o bilhete; **~ machine** a máquina de venda de bilhetes; **~ office** a bilheteria
tie (clothing) a gravata
time as horas
timetable [BE] o horário
tire o pneu
tired cansado, cansada
tissue o lenço de papel
today hoje
toe o dedo do pé
together juntos
toilet a casa de banho
toilet paper o papel higênico
tomorrow amanhã

tongue a língua
tonight hoje à noite; **for ~** para hoje à noite
too (much) demasiado; **(also)** também
tooth o dente
toothbrush a escova de dentes
toothpaste a pasta de dentes
tour a visita
tourist o/a turista
towel a toalha
town a cidade; **~ hall** a câmara municipal; **~ map** o mapa de cidade
toy o brinquedo
toy store a loja de brinquedos
track o trilho
traffic o trânsito; **~ jam** o engarrafamento; **~ circle** o balão; **~ light** o semáforo
trail o caminho; **~ map** o mapa
train o trem; **~ station** a estação ferroviária
transfer (plane, train) a conexão
translate *v* traduzir
trash o lixo; **~ can** a lixeira
travel *v* viajar; **~ agency** a agência de viagens
traveler's check o cheque de viagens
tree a árvore
trip a excursão
trolley o carrinho
trousers [BE] as calças
T-shirt a T-Shirt [a camiseta]
TV a televisão [a TV]
type o tipo
tyre [BE] o pneu

U

ugly feio, feia
umbrella (rain) o guarda-chuva
unbranded medication [BE] o medicamento genérico
uncle o tio
unconscious perder os sentidos
underground [BE] o metrô; **~ station [BE]** a estação de metrô
underpants as cuecas
understand compreende
United Kingdom o Reino Unido
United States os Estados Unidos
university a universidade
unleaded (gas) sem chumbo
unlimited (mileage) sem limite (de quilometragem)
unlock *v* abrir
upper superior
upstairs em cima
use *v* usar
use *n* uso

useful útil
username o nome de usuário
utensil o utensílio

V

vacancy o quarto vago
vacation as férias
vaccination a vacinação
vacuum cleaner o aspirador
vagina a vagina
valid válido
valley o vale
valuable de valor
value o valor
VAT (sales tax) IVA
vegetarian vegetariano
vehicle o veículo; **~ registration** os documentos do carro
veterinarian o veterinário a veterinária
view point [BE] o mirante
village a aldeia
vineyard o vinhedo
visa o visto
visit *n* a visita
visit *v* visitar
visitor center o centro de informações turísticas
visually impaired os deficientes visuais
vitamin a vitamina
volleyball o voleibol
vomit vomitar

W

wait esperar
waiting room a sala de espera
waiter o garçom
waitress a garçonete
wake-up call a chamada para despertar
walk *v* dar um passeio a pé
walking passear a pé
walking route o roteiro para caminhada
wall a parede
wallet a carteira (de documentos)
warm *adj* morno, morna; *v* aquecer
wash *v* lavar
washing machine a máquina de lavar
watch *n* o relógio; *v* ver
water a água
water skis os esquis aquáticos
weather o tempo; **~ forecast** a previsão do tempo
wedding o casamento; **~ ring** a aliança de casamento
week a semana
weekend o fim de semana
weekly (ticket) (bilhete) semanal

welcome bem-vindo (m), bem-vinda (f)
west oeste
what o que
wheelchair a cadeira de rodas; **~ ramp** a rampa para cadeira de rodas
when quando
where onde
white branco, branca
who quem
wife a esposa
window a janela; **(store)** a vitrine
window seat o lugar à janela
windshield o para-brisas
windsurfer a prancha à vela
wireless sem fio; **~ internet** internet sem fio; **~ internet service** serviçode internet sem fio; **~ phone** telefhone sem fio
with com
without sem
woman a mulher
wool a lã
work *v* **(job)** trabalhar; **(function)** funcionar
wrap *v* embrulhar
wrist o pulso
write *v* escrever
wrong errado, errada

Y

year o ano
yellow amarelo, amarela
yes sim
young jovem
youth hostel o albergue da juventude

Z

zebra crossing [BE] a faixa de pedestres
zero zero
zone a zona
zoo o zoológico

Brazilian Portuguese–English

A

à tarde p.m.
a abadia abbey
o abajur lampshade
aberto open
o abraço hug
abril April
acampar camp
o acesso para deficientes access for handicapped
os achados e perdidos lost and found
o açougue butcher
o acrílico acrylic
o açúcar sugar
adiante ahead
as entradas/inscrições admissions
o advogado attorney
o aeroporto airport
a agência de câmbio currency exchange office
a agência de viagens travel agent
agora now
agosto August
a água potável drinking water
o albergue de juventude youth hostel
a aldeia village
a alergia allergy
alérgico allergic
a alfândega customs
o algodão cotton
alguém someone
os alimentos naturais health food
o alojamento accommodations
alpinismo mountaineering
aluga-se for rent
alugam-se carros car rental
aluguel de bicicletas bicycle rental
amanhã tomorrow
a ambulância ambulance
antiguidades antiques
aquecer warm
área para fumantes smoking (area)
a areia sand
o aspirador vacuum
o assento seat
o assento à janela window seat
o assento no corredor aisle seat
a assinatura signature
atender answer
o atendimento admissions
o atendimento ao cliente customer service
atrasado delayed
automático automatic
o automóvel car

o avião plane
o aviso warning

B

a bagagem baggage [luggage]
o balão traffic circle [roundabout]
o balcão de registo check-in counter
o balcão de informações information desk
a balsa ferry
a bancade jornais newsagent
o banco bank
o banheiro bathroom [toilets]
a banheira bath
o barbeiro barber
o barco boat
o barco salva-vidas lifeboat
o basebol baseball
o basquetebol basketball
o beijo kiss
benvindo welcome
a biblioteca library
a bicicleta bicycle
a bicicleta de montanha mountain bike
o bilhete eletrônico e-ticket
o bilhete semanal weekly ticket
a bilheteria ticket office
o bilhete ticket
os bolsos pockets
a bomba pump
os bombeiros fire department [brigade]
o bonde tram
as botas de esqui ski boots
o boxe boxing

C

o cabeleireiro hairdresser
o cabelo hair
a cachoeira waterfall
a cadeira de rodas wheelchair
o café da manhã breakfast
a caixa cashier
o calçado shoes
acalculadora calculator
o calor heat
as calorias calories
a câmara municipal municipal town hall
o caminhão truck
o caminho path
o camping campsite
o campo de esportes playing field
o canal canal
cancelado canceled
o capacete helmet
a capela chapel
o cardápio menu
o carnaval carnival
a carne meat
o carro car

a carta registrada registered letter
o cartão de visitas business card
a carteira wallet
a casa house
o casaco coat
o castelo castle
a catedral cathedral
o cavalo horse
a caverna cave
o cemitério cemetery
o centavo cent
o centro da cidade downtown area
o centro esportivo sports center
a cerveja beer
o chá tea
o chalé cottage
a chamada gratuita toll-free call
a chave key
as chegadas arrivals (airport)
a chupeta pacifier
o churrasco barbecue
a chuva rain
o chuveiro shower
a cidade city
a cidade antiga old town
o cigarro cigarette
o cinema movie theater [cinema]
a cirurgia surgery
a clínica de saúde health clinic
o cobre copper
o código code
o código de área area code
o colete salva-vidas life jacket
a colina hill
com with
com chumbo leaded
o combustível fuel
completo full
o comprimido pill
o computador computer
a comunhão communion
o condicionador conditioner
a confeitaria pastry shop
congelado frozen
os consertos repairs
a conta corrente checking [current] account
a conta de poupança savings account
o conteúdo contents
o controle de passaportes passport control
o(s) correio(s) post office
o correio normal regular mail
o correio rápido express mail
o cadeado lock
o corpo de bombeiros fire station
os cosméticos cosmetics
a costa coast
o couro leather
o cartão telefônico phone card
a criança child

o cuidado caution
os cuidados intensivos intensive care

D

a dança dance
a data date
a data de nascimento date of birth
de ida e volta round-trip [return]
a delegacia de polícia police station
o dentista dentist
a depilação a cera waxing
o depósito de bagagem baggage check
descartável disposable
o desconto discount
desembarque arrivals (airport)
o desentupidor plunger
o deserto desert
despachar check (baggage)
o destino destination
o desvio detour [diversion]
o detergente detergent
devagar slow
Dezembro December
dia de Ano Novo New Year's Day
os dias úteis weekdays
os dicionários dictionaries
a dieta diet
digital digital
o dique dam
dirija com cuidado drive carefully
dissolver dissolve
a distância distance
os doces candy [sweets]
os documentos do carro car registration papers
os documentos de registro registration papers
doméstico domestic
domingo Sunday
a dor pain
a drogaria drugstore
a duna dune

E

o elevador elevator
em construção under construction
em uso, ocupado occupied
a embaixada embassy
o embarque departures (airport)
a emergência emergency
empurrar push
a encosta perigosa dangerous slope
o endereço address
a enseada bay
a entrada entrance
a entrada proibida no entry
entrar enter

a entrega de bagagem baggage claim
as entregas deliveries
o equipamento de mergulho diving equipment
os equipamentos eletrônicos electronic goods
a escada rolante escalator
as escadas stairs
escalar climbing
a escola school
o escritório office
a especialidade da casa house specialty
a especialidade da região local specialty
o espectáculo show
o espectador spectator
o esporte sports
o esqui aquático waterskiing
a esquiagem skiing
os esquis skis
os esquis aquáticos water skis
esta noite this evening
a estação station
a estação de trem train station
a estação de metrô subway [underground] station
a estação ferroviária train station
a estação rodoviária bus [coach] station
estacionamento parking deck [car park]
o estacionamento para clientes customer parking
estacione aqui park here
o estádio stadium
a estância turística tourist resort
o estanho can
a estátua statue
a estrada road
a estrada em construção road under construction
a estrada fechada road closed
o estrangeiro foreign
a estreia premiere
o estuário estuary
exclusivo para residentes residents only
exclusivo para pedestres pedestrians only
exclusivo para pessoal autorizado authorized vehicles only
a excursão tour
exige-se a identificação proof of identity required
a exposição exhibition
o extintor (de incêndios) fire extinguisher

F

a fábrica factory
a faixa de ônibus bus lane
a faixa de pedestres crosswalk [zebra crossing]
fala-se inglês English spoken
a falésia cliff
a farmácia drugstore
o farol lighthouse
a fazenda farm
a febre fever
fechado closed
a feira fair
feito à mão handmade
o feriado nacional national holiday
o a ferrovia railroad
Fevereiro February
o fim end
o fim da rodovia end of highway [motorway]
a floresta forest
o/a florista florist
o fogo de artifício fireworks
a fonte fountain
a forma form
a fortaleza fortress
o forte fort
a fotocópia photocopy
a fotografia photography
a fralda diaper [nappy]
o freio brake
o freio de emergência emergency brake
a frente front
fresco fresh
a fronteira border crossing
a fruta fruit
fumar *v* smoke
o futebol soccer [football]
o futebol americano American football

G

a galeria de arte art gallery
a garagem garage
a garantia guarantee
a gasolina gas [petrol]
genuino genuine
o/a gerente manager
o ginásio gym
o glúten gluten
o golfe golf
a gota drop
gracioso cute
grande large
grátis free
gratuito free
a gravata tie
a grávida pregnant
a grelha de churrasco barbecue
o grelhado grilled

a gruta cave
o guarda chuva umbrella
guardar save
o guia turístico tourist guide
o guia de viagem travel guide

H

o handebol handball
o helicóptero helicopter
o hipismo horseback riding
o hipódromo racetrack [racecourse]
hoje today
o hóquei hockey
o hóquei no gelo ice hockey
o horário schedule [timetable]
o horário comercial business hours
o horário de abertura opening hours
o horário de visitas visiting hours
o hospital hospital
o hotel hotel

I

ida e volta round-trip [return]
a igreja church
a ilha island
a impressão printing
incluído included
incluído no preço included in the price
as informações information
as informações turísticas tourist information
o ingrediente ingredient
o início de rodovia highway [motorway] entrance
inocente innocent
inquebrável unbreakable
inserir *v* insert
insosso bland
as instruções instructions
integral whole wheat
interdito ao trânsito traffic-free zone
interessado interested
internacional international
introduzir introduce
o inverno winter
o IVA imposto de venda agregada sales tax [VAT]

J

lâmina de barbear razor
Janeiro January
a janela window
o jardim garden
o jardim botânico botanical garden
o jardim de infância kindergarten
a joalheria jeweler
o jogo match
Julho July

Junho June

L

a lã wool
o lago lake
a lancha a motor motorboat
os lanches snacks
a lanterna lamp
os laticínios dairy products
a lavagem de carros car wash
a lavagem de roupa laundry facilities
a lavanderia laundromat [launderette]
a lavanderia a seco dry-cleaner
lavar a seco dry-clean only
lavável à máquina machine washable
a lembrança souvenir
a lente lens
as lições lessons
o limite da cidade city limits
o limite de bagagem baggage allowance
a limpeza cleaning
a língua language
a língua estrangeira foreign language
a linha platform
a linha aérea airline
a linha de bonde tram
a linha férrea railroad [railway]
a linha de pesca fishing rod
a liquidação clearance sale
o líquido liquid
Lisboa Lisbon
a lista telefónica directory
a lista de preços price list
o litoral coast
a livraria bookstore
livre vacant
a lixa nail file
o loção pós-barba after-shave lotion
a loja de alimentos naturais health food store
a loja de antiguidades antique store
a loja de artigos de esporte sporting goods store
a loja de brinquedos toy store
a loja de conveniência delicatessen
a loja de departamento department store
as lojas duty-free duty-free store
esgotado sold out
a loteria lottery
a louça china
o luxo luxury
as luzes highlights

M

a madeira wood
o maestro conductor
Maio May
mais more
mais devagar slower
mais rápido faster
a mamadeira baby bottle
mandar send
os mandriões loafers
o mapa da cidade city map
o mapa dos arredores area map
a máquina fotográfica camera
o mar sea
Março March
as massas noodles
a mata wood
a maternidade maternity
o médico doctor
médio medium
o menu menu
o menu turístico tourist menu
o mercado market
as mercadorias goods
as mercadorias isentas de impostos duty-free goods
a mercearia grocer
mergulhar diving
o metrô subway [underground]
a mina mine
a missa mass
o mobiliário furniture
a moeda coin
o moinho mill
o moinho de vento windmill
molhada wet
o molusco shellfish
a montanha mountain
o montanhismo mountaineering
o monte hill
o monumento monument
o monumento comemorativo (war) memorial
o mosteiro monastery
a moto motorcycle
os móveis furniture
as mudanças manual shift
a troca de óleo oil change
mudar change
a mulher woman
a muralha da cidade city wall
o muro wall
o museu museum
a música music
a música ao vivo live music
a música clássica classical music
a música folk folk music
a música pop pop music

N

nacional national
nacionalidade nationality

nada a declarar nothing to declare
não entre keep out
não fumadores non-smokers
não fumantes non-smokers
não fumar no smoking
não funciona out of order
não-retornável non-returnable
o Natal Christmas
navegação à vela sailing
o navio ship
a neve snow
o nome name
a nome de família last name
o nome de solteira maiden name
Novembro November
novo new
as nozes nuts
o número de telefone telephone number
o número do passaporte passport number

O

as obras construction
o oculista optician
ocupado, em uso occupied
a oferta especial special offer
o óleo oil
o ônibus bus [coach]
o operador operator
a ordem de pagamento money order
a orquestra orchestra
a ourivesaria goldsmith
o ouro gold
o outono fall [autumn]
Outubro October

P

o paço palace
a padaria bakery
o país country
o palácio palace
o palácio da justiça law court
o palco stage
o pão bread
o papel higiênico toilet paper
o papel reciclado recycled paper
a papelaria stationery store
para microondas microwaveable
para uso externo external use only
a parada de ônibus bus stop
o parapente gliding
o pára-quedas parachuting
pare stop
a parede wall
o parque park
o parque de campismo campsite
o parque de diversões amusement park
o parque de estacionamento parking lot [car park]

o parque nacional national park
o parque para clientes customer parking
o parque privativo private parking
as partidas departures (airport)
as partidas internacionais international departures
a Páscoa Easter
o passageiro passenger
as passagens (airplane) tickets
o passaporte passport
o passe mensal monthly ticket
o passeio walkway
o passeio panorâmico scenic route
o passeio a cavalo horseback riding
o passeio com guia guided tour
o passeio circular round trip
a pastilha lozenge
a patinação no gelo ice skating
os patins skates
o patrimônio do estado public (building)
o pedágio toll
pedestre pedestrian
o pediatra pediatrician
a pedicure pedicure
o peito chest
peixaria fish store [fishmonger]
a pensão bed & breakfast
o pedestre pedestrian
pequeno small
o percurso da natureza nature trail
o percurso de bicicleta bike trail
o percurso panorâmico scenic route
perdido lost
o perigo danger
perigoso dangerous
permanecer *v* stay
a pérola pearl
perto near
a pesca fishing
o pico peak
a pílula pill
o PIN PIN
a piscina swimming pool
a pista de corrida racetrack
a pista de ônibus bus lane
pista escorregadia slippery road surface
a pista fechada road closed
a pista simples two-way traffic
a placa do carro license plate [registration] number
o planador gliding
o planetário planetarium
as plataformas platforms
o pneu tire [tyre]
o poço well
pode cozinhar cooking facilities

a polícia police
a polícia de trânsito traffic police
a pomada ointment
o pomar orchard
a ponte bridge
a ponte baixa low bridge
a ponte estreita narrow bridge
a ponte levadiça drawbridge
o ponto de ônibus bus stop
o ponto de táxi taxi stand [rank]
por favor please
a porta door
o porta-moedas purse
a porta de embarque boarding gate
a porta de incêndio fire door
o portão gate
a porta automática automatic door
o porto port
o posto de ambulância ambulance station
o posto de gasolina gas [petrol] station
a pousada guest house
o povoado village
a praça town square
a praia beach
a praia de nudismo nudist beach
a prancha de surf[e] surfboard
a prata silver
o prato do dia dish of the day
o preço price
a primavera spring
o primeiro andar first floor
a primeira classe first class
o primeiro nome first name
os primeiros socorros first aid
a prioridade priority
prisão de ventre constipated
privado private
os produtos de limpeza cleaning products
proibida a entrada no entry
proibido forbidden
proibido acampar no camping
proibido estacionar no parking
proibido fumar no smoking
a promoção sale
o pronto socorro-emergência accident and emergency
o propósito purpose
provar *v* taste
o próximo next
puxar pull

Q

a quantia fare
quarta-feira Wednesday
o quarto de casal double room
o quarto para alugar room to rent
quatro estrelas four star

a queda de pedras falling rocks
o quilometro kilometer
quinta-feira Thursday

R

os raios-x x-ray
a rampa ramp
a recepção reception
o recibo receipt
reciclado recycled
reduza a velocidade slow down
o reembolso refund
as refeições meals
o regente conductor (music)
a região region
o relicário shrine
a represa dam
reservado reserved
a reserva reservation
o reservatório reservoir
residencial guest house
o restaurante restaurant
retirada de dinheiro withdraw money
retire o bilhete take ticket
retornar v return
a revista magazine
a ribeira stream
o rio river
o rochedo cliff
a rodovia highway [motorway]
o rolo film (camera)
a rota alternada alternate route
roupa íntima underwear
a rua street
rua estreita narrow road
a rua fechada ao trânsito road closed
a rua principal main road
a rua com sentido único one-way street
as ruinas ruins

S

sábado Saturday
o sabonete soap
o saco bag
a saída exit
a saída de emergência emergency exit
o sal salt
a sala de operações operating room
a sala de concertos concert hall
a sala de espera waiting room
o salva-vidas lifeguards
o sapato shoe
a sé cathedral
o secador de cabelo hair dryer
a seda silk
a segunda classe second class
o segundo andar second floor

segunda-feira Monday
os segundos seconds
a segurança security
o seguro insurance
o selo stamp
sem açúcar sugar-free
sem álcool alcohol-free
sem cafeína caffeine-free
sem chumbo unleaded
sem gordura fat-free
sem sal salt-free
o semáforo traffic light
a semana week
a senha ticket
as senhoras ladies
a serra mountain range
o serviço service charge
o serviço a clientes customer service
o serviço de emergência emergency serviceso
o serviço de quarto room service
o serviço incluído service included
Setembro September
sexta-feira Friday
o shopping center shopping mall [shopping centre]
o silêncio silence
a sinaleira traffic light
só com dinheiro cash only
a sobremesa dessert
a soirée evening performance
o solário sun lounge
a sopa soup
o spa spa
o suco fruit juice
o supermercado supermarket

T

os talheres utensils [cutlery]
a tarifa rate
a tarifa de pedágio toll
a tarifa mínima minimum charge
a taxa de serviço service charge
o táxi taxi
o taxímetro taxi meter
o teatro theater
o teatro ao ar livrea open-air theater
o teatro infantil children´s theater
o teleférico chair lift
o telefone telephone
o telefone de emergência emergency telephone
o telefone público public telephone
o telefone residencial home phone number
os temperos spices
a tenda tent
o tênis tennis
a terapia intensiva intensive care

terça-feira Tuesday
o terminal terminal
tinta fresca wet paint
as toalhas linen
tóxico toxic
o tráfego lento slow traffic
o trailer/reboque trailer
o trajeto de ônibus bus route
o trampolim diving board
transferir transfer
o trânsito impedido closed to traffic
transportar carry
o tratamento treatment
o trem expresso express train
o trem local local train
o trem metropolitano local train
o trem rápido express train
trevo, cruzamento intersection
o trigo wheat
o túmulo grave
o túnel tunnel
o turismo tourist information office

U

a universidade university
os utensílios de cozinha kitchen equipment
os utensílios domésticos household goods

V

o vagão-leito sleeping car
o vagão restaurante dining car
a vaga vacancy
vago vacant
o vale valley
o vale postal money order
válido valid
a varanda balcony
os vegetais vegetables
o veículo vehicle
o veículo lento slow vehicle
o veleiro sailboat
a velocidade máxima maximum speed limit
venenoso poisonous
o verão summer
o verdadeiro real
o verdureiro fruit and vegetable store
o vestuário fitting room
a via de dois sentidos two-way traffic
a via de sentido único one-way street
a via turística scenic route
o vidro glass
o vidro reciclado recycled glass
a vila town
o vilarejo village
as vinhas vineyard

o vinho do porto port (wine)
o vinho wine
a visita guiada guided tour
o voleibol volleyball
o vôo flight

Z

o zoológico a zoo
aduaneira customs zone
a zona a zone
a zona comercial business district
a zona de pedestres pedestrian zone
a zona histórica historic area
a zona residencial residential zone
zero zero

Berlitz®

speaking your language

phrase book & dictionary
phrase book & CD

Available in: Arabic, Burmese*, Cantonese Chinese, Croatian, Czech*, Danish*, Dutch, English, Filipino, Finnish*, French, German, Greek, Hebrew*, Hindi*, Hungarian*, Indonesian, Italian, Japanese, Korean, Latin American Spanish, Malay, Mandarin Chinese, Mexican Spanish, Norwegian, Polish, Portuguese, Romanian*, Russian, Spanish, Swedish, Thai, Turkish, Vietnamese

*Book only

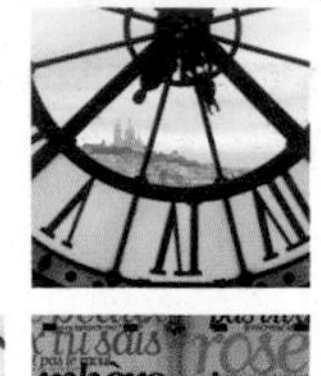

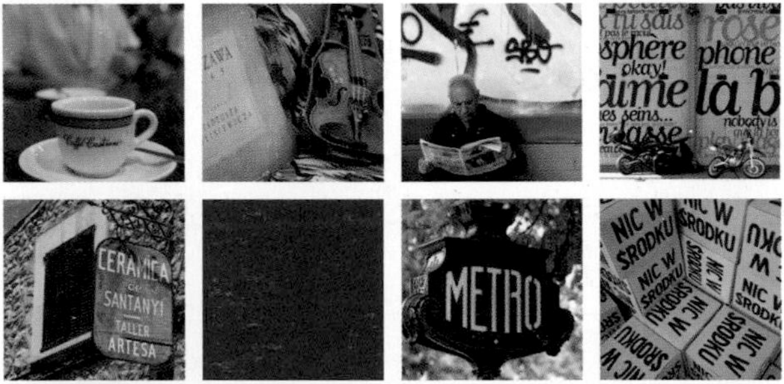

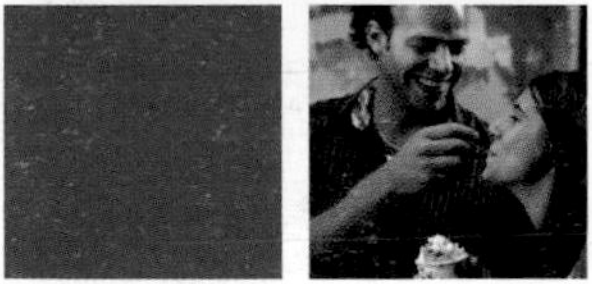

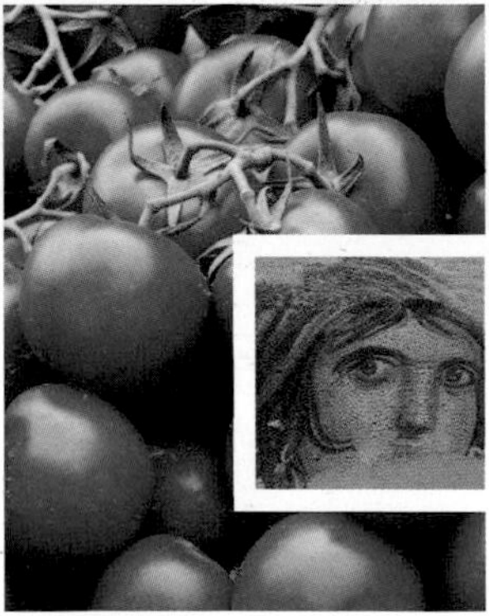

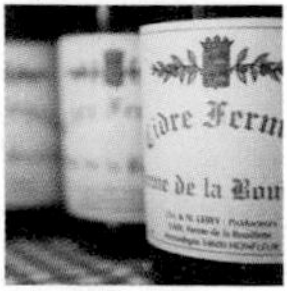